THE SMART INVESTOR'S GUIDE TO MACROECONOMICS

Dan Hartshorn

INTRODUCTION

Macroeconomics is a branch of economics that studies the performance, structure, behavior, and decision-making of the overall economy. It is concerned with the aggregate changes in the economy such as unemployment, growth rate, gross domestic product (GDP), and inflation.

Macroeconomics is a broad field that covers a wide range of topics, including economic growth and development, inflation, interest rates, unemployment, consumer confidence, fiscal and monetary policy, business cycles, financial markets, and public finance. Macroeconomics is a complex field of study that is constantly evolving as new theories and data are developed. By understanding how the economy works, macroeconomics can help us to make better decisions about our lives and our future.

This book isn't for economists. It is for the average investor, those of us who are interested in investing our money tactically and wisely. On my investment journey, I've become fascinated with macroeconomic indicators and have recognized that the more I understand them, the better able I am to make smarter choices about how I invest my capital.

Whether it's understanding the phases of the business cycle of the economy, how rising or falling inflation can impact which investments are favorable, or how changing interest rates can impact different assets, macroeconomics can help investors make wise decisions. How do fluctuations in the housing market inform investors about not only real estate investment, but impacts across different types of assets and commodities? How can the stock market be viewed as a sensitive and dynamic indicator of the broader economic ecosystem? We'll take a look at all these ideas.

Two topics at the forefront of this book are investing and risk management. Putting money to work so that it can grow over time and protecting these financial assets from unexpected events are critical activities to learn. Investing and risk management strategies can be more expertly employed when coupled with a wider view that includes macroeconomic trends.

So how exactly do macroeconomics and investing and risk management relate? How can knowledge of macroeconomics benefit an investor who is looking to invest smarter and control risk? For one, macroeconomic factors can help you identify potential investment opportunities. For example, if you believe that the economy is headed for a period of growth, you might invest in stocks or other assets that are expected to benefit from that growth. Next, macroeconomic factors can also help investors manage risk. For example, if you are concerned about inflation, you may want to invest in assets that are less sensitive to inflation, such as real estate or commodities. Finally, macroeconomic factors can help investors decide when to invest and when to wait. For example, if you believe that the economy is about to enter a recession, you might sell some investments and wait until the economy recovers before buying again.

Many specific macroeconomic factors can inform the smart investor in a variety of ways. Economic growth, the rate at which the economy is expanding, can create more opportunities for businesses and investors, which can lead to higher asset prices. Inflation, the rate at which prices are rising, can erode the value of assets. Interest rates, the cost of borrowing money, can make it more expensive for businesses to invest and for consumers to borrow money, which can slow economic growth. Unemployment, the percentage of the labor force that is unemployed, can lead to lower asset prices as businesses and consumers have less money to spend. By understanding these macroeconomic factors, you can make better decisions about your investments and develop effective risk management strategies.

Before we dive in, I'll tell you a little bit about myself. I'm a career engineer and I work at a large manufacturing company in the US. I'm less than a decade from retirement and as I've gotten older I've become more interested in investing. One of the best financial decisions I ever made was to direct a portion of my paycheck directly to a 401K account. I started doing this over twenty years ago when I started my career and over time it has grown steadily. I can't encourage you enough to start this practice as early as possible. It's particularly helpful when you work for a company that will match a percentage of your contributions.

As an engineer, I'm accustomed to seeking answers, solving mysteries, pursuing research, and answering tough questions. Over time I've become more interested in economics and taking a more active role in my investment strategy. Using my engineering mindset, I set out to learn all I can about investment strategy and I found macroeconomics to be fascinating. I have enjoyed learning over time about how broader economic indicators can help inform me about specific investment choices. The more I learn, the more tactical my investment decisions become and I've very much enjoyed the process. I wanted to put some of this knowledge together in one place, and this book has grown out of my notes and journals of my exploration of topics in macroeconomics and specifically how they relate to my investment strategy.

Finally, it is necessary to be clear about an important matter. While this book provides an in-depth exploration of macroeconomic indicators and how savvy investors analyze them, it should not be misconstrued as personalized financial or investment advice. The educational material and entertainment perspectives represented are intended to provide the reader with helpful conceptual frameworks for thinking about the economy and markets. However, every individual's financial situation and risk tolerances are unique. Specific investment decisions should be made in consultation with licensed financial advisors who can tailor recommendations directly to one's complete financial picture and goals. The author and publisher do not assume liability for how readers apply the general information contained herein, which is provided for entertainment and educational purposes only. All investing carries inherent risks, and there are no guarantees any concepts discussed will prove profitable. Please use your best judgment and consult appropriate experts before making major investment choices.

CHAPTER 1:
ECONOMIC GROWTH

I magine that a baker opens a small shop in your neighborhood. She works hard and has a talent for baking tasty sourdough bread and hearty wheat bread with a thick and crunchy crust. She gets up very early so that when people in the neighborhood leave to go to work, she has steaming hot slices of bread and butter and jam ready for everybody to enjoy. Her business is a hit and more people learn of it by word of mouth. Folks buy fresh loaves of bread and bring it into the office to share and it becomes more popular. Soon, the baker has so much business that she hires some workers to help her produce more bread. She expands her menu to include white bread, rye, and raisin bread. Soon she buys a larger store and expands her kitchen from two to six ovens and her business continues to grow. This is an example of economic growth.

Economic growth in the economy is the increase in the production of goods and services over time. Growth can happen for different reasons. New technology that makes it easier or less expensive to produce goods can spur growth. If workers become more skilled or have better tools to work with, they can produce more goods and services in the same amount of time. If the population grows or more people enter the workforce, there will be more people to produce goods and services.

The economy moves through a business cycle that can be broken into four different phases: expansion, peak, contraction, and trough. During the expansion phase, production and sales of goods and services increase. The number of people who are employed increases. Businesses are more likely to hire more people and develop new products. Oftentimes income levels rise, causing people to spend more money in the economy. This leads to increased demand for goods and services, which further fuels economic growth.

Once the expansion phase slows, it hits a peak which can last for some time. Inevitably, what follows is a contraction, which is a period of economic decline. Businesses begin cutting costs, possibly laying off workers and they spend less money on product development. People spend less money which further puts pressure on businesses. If a contraction is prolonged it can eventually turn into a recession. Governments and central banks can take steps to try to mitigate the effects of a contraction. For example, they may cut taxes or interest rates to stimulate the economy. Eventually, a contraction will reach its end in the final phase of the business cycle called a trough. This is the lowest point of economic decline after which a new expansion begins.

That's the general flow of the business cycle and it's measured from peak to peak or trough to trough. It can be more complex, as there may be shorter periods of contraction during long periods of expansion, but that's the general idea. Economic growth can be measured in different ways, but the most common measure is the GDP.

The gross domestic product (GDP) is a measure of the total value of goods and services produced in a country or region in a given period. It is often used as a measure of the size of an economy. It is used by governments, businesses, and economists to track the health of an economy and to make decisions about economic policy.

The concept of GDP was first developed by Simon Kuznets in the 1930s. Kuznets was an American economist who was interested in measuring the size and growth of the US economy. He developed a method of calculating GDP that is still used today.

Kuznets was born in Pinsk, Belarus, in 1901. He immigrated to the United States in 1922 and earned a Ph.D. in economics from Columbia University in 1926. He then worked as a research economist at the National Bureau of Economic Research (NBER) for over 30 years.

At the NBER, Kuznets developed the concept of GDP and helped to develop the first estimates of GDP for the United States. He also researched economic growth, income inequality, and the distribution of wealth.

Kuznets' work on GDP has had a profound impact on the way economists measure and understand economic activity. GDP is now used by governments, businesses, and economists around the world to track the health of economies and to make decisions about economic policy.

In addition to his work on GDP, Kuznets also made significant contributions to the field of economic history. He was the first economist to systematically study the long-term patterns of economic growth and development. His work on economic history has helped us to understand the factors that contribute to economic growth and the challenges that developing countries face. In 1971, Kuznets received the Nobel Memorial Prize in Economic Sciences.

The way GDP is calculated has changed over time. In the early days, GDP was only calculated for the production of goods. Services were not included until the 1960s. GDP is now calculated to include all goods and services produced in an economy. The way GDP is measured also varies from country to country. Some countries use different methods of calculating GDP than others, which can make it difficult to compare GDP estimates between countries.

There are many different uses of the GDP. It's used to track the growth of an economy, measuring how quickly an economy is expanding or contracting. It is used as a benchmark to compare the size of different countries' economies. GDP can help assess the health of an economy. For example, a low GDP growth rate may indicate that an economy is struggling. Governments use the GDP to make economic policy decisions. A government may increase spending if the GDP is low.

The GDP is a useful measure of the size of an economy, but it has some limitations. For instance, it doesn't take into account the distribution of income or wealth in an economy. Additionally, GDP can be affected by factors that are not related to economic activity, such as natural disasters or wars.

An understanding of economic growth, the business cycle, and GDP can help inform your investment decisions in several ways. By understanding the current state of the economy, you can make better decisions about which assets to invest in. During a period of expansion, when GDP is growing, you may be more likely to invest in stocks or other assets that are expected to benefit from economic growth. During a period of contraction, when GDP is declining, you might invest in assets that are less risky, such as bonds or cash.

Let's take a closer look at some of the specific investments that may be more appealing during periods of expansion in the business cycle. Stocks are shares of ownership in a company. When a company does well, the value of its stock typically goes up. So, if you believe that the economy is going to grow, you may want to invest in stocks. Real estate is another asset that tends to do well during periods of economic growth. As the economy grows, more people can afford to buy homes and businesses. This demand for real estate can drive up prices. Commodities are another investment to consider during periods of expansion. Commodities are raw materials, such as oil, gold, and wheat. Commodity prices tend to go up when the economy is growing, as businesses need more raw materials to produce goods and services.

On the other hand, some investments may be more appealing during periods of contraction in the business cycle. Bonds are loans that you make to a company or government. When you buy a bond, you are essentially lending money to that entity. Bonds are considered to be relatively safe investments, as the borrower is legally obligated to repay you the money you lent them, plus interest. Short-term investments are investments that mature in less than one year. These investments are typically less risky than long-term investments, such as stocks and real estate. Cash is the most liquid asset, meaning that it can be easily converted into other assets. During periods of economic decline, you may want to hold more cash so that you can easily access your money if needed.

By understanding the future outlook for the economy, you can make better decisions about when to invest, when to save, and when to sell. If GDP is expected to grow, you may be more likely to invest in shorter-term investments. If GDP is in decline, you might invest in longer-term investments.

Some examples of short-term investments include high-yield savings accounts, money market accounts, certificates of deposit (CDs), treasury bills, money market mutual funds, and peer-to-peer lending. When choosing a short-term investment, it's important to consider your individual needs and goals. If quick access to money is needed, a high-yield savings account or money market account may be a good option. If on the other hand, a higher interest rate is sought, a CD or Treasury bill may be a better choice. And if you're willing to take on some risk, peer-to-peer lending can be a way to earn higher returns. It's also important to remember that short-term investments typically offer lower returns than long-term investments.

Examples of long-term investments include stocks, bonds, mutual funds, exchange-traded funds (ETFs), real estate, pension plans, and annuities. Depending on your situation, different types of long-term investments may make more sense. If you're saving for retirement, you may want to consider a mix of stocks, bonds, and mutual funds. If you are looking for a more conservative investment, real estate or annuities might serve better. It's also important to remember that long-term investments are subject to market risk. This means that the value of an investment can go down as well as up. So it's important to invest for the long term and not panic if the market takes a downturn.

By understanding the relationship between GDP and other economic factors, such as inflation and interest rates, you can make better decisions about how to manage your risk. If GDP is growing and inflation is low, you may be more likely to take on more risk.

Let's look at some examples of some higher-risk investments that might be appealing in this situation. Growth stocks are stocks of companies that are expected to grow their earnings at a faster rate than the overall market. These stocks can be more volatile than other types of stocks, but they also have the potential to generate higher returns. Small-cap stocks are stocks of companies with market capitalizations of less than $2 billion. Small-cap stocks are considered to be more risky than large-cap stocks, but they also have the potential for higher returns. Emerging market stocks are stocks of companies in developing countries. Emerging markets are often characterized by strong economic growth, but they can also be more volatile than developed markets.

Venture capital is a type of investment that is made in early-stage companies. Venture capital investments are considered to be high-risk, but they also have the potential for high returns. Commodities are raw materials, such as oil, gold, or wheat.

Commodity prices can be volatile, making them a high-risk investment. However, commodities can also be a good way to hedge against inflation. Finally, foreign exchange (FX) trading is the buying and selling of currencies. FX trading can be a high-risk investment, but it can also be a way to profit from changes in currency exchange rates.

If GDP is declining and inflation is high, you may be more likely to take on less risk. Several types of investments could be appealing in this macroeconomic situation. Some examples are money market funds, certificates of deposit (CDs), treasury inflation-protected securities (TIPS), high-quality bonds, real estate, and dividend stocks. We'll look more closely at these types of investments in the next chapter on inflation.

CHAPTER 2: INFLATION

L et's visit our neighborhood baker again. Unfortunately, the economy has entered a period of contraction. The baker buys wheat flour, cultures for sourdough, rye, raisins, sugar, and other ingredients to produce her bread. The prices of these items have been increasing and soon she has no choice but to raise the prices she charges for hot, delicious bread. You're a big fan of her bread and you understand that times are getting tougher for everyone. You pay more money for the same bread that you've been enjoying all these months.

Inflation is a general increase in prices and a decrease in the purchasing value of money. When the general price level rises, each unit of currency buys fewer goods and services. In other words, inflation reflects a decrease in the purchasing power of money.

Inflation can be caused by several factors, including increased demand, increased costs, government spending, and expectations.

Increased demand is when there is more demand for goods and services than there is supply. When this happens prices will rise. This is because businesses can charge more for their products and services when there are more buyers than sellers. There is a good example of this in recent US history.

The late 1960s and early 1970s were turbulent times for the US economy. The US fiscal situation was strained by the Vietnam War and President Johnson's Great Society legislation, a set of expensive domestic programs aimed at eliminating poverty and racial injustice. Repeated energy crises that increased oil costs and sapped US growth disrupted the economy. The first crisis was an Arab oil embargo that began in October 1973 and lasted about five months. During this period, crude oil prices quadrupled to a plateau that held until the Iranian revolution brought a second energy crisis in 1979. The second crisis tripled the cost of oil.

The rise in oil prices caused a sharp increase in inflation. This was because the increase in oil prices led to an increase in the cost of production for many goods and services. Businesses had to pass these higher costs on to consumers in the form of higher prices.

The increase in oil prices also led to a decrease in economic growth. This was because the higher oil prices made it more expensive for businesses to operate, which led to layoffs and a decrease in investment.

The oil crises of the 1970s are a good example of how increased demand for a product can contribute to inflation. When the oil demand increased, the price of oil also increased. This increase in the price of oil then led to an increase in the cost of production for many goods and services, which in turn led to an increase in inflation.

Another factor that can contribute to inflation is increased costs, which occur when the costs of production rise. Businesses may pass those costs on to consumers in the form of higher prices. This can happen if, for example, the price of raw materials or labor increases. This is also known as cost-push inflation. One famous example of this in recent history happened in what was then the Soviet Union.

In the 1970s, the Soviet Union experienced a series of crop failures that led to sharp increases in the price of food. These crop failures were caused by a combination of factors, including drought, poor farming practices, and government policies.

The drought was the most significant factor. In 1972, the Soviet Union experienced its worst drought in 50 years. This drought led to widespread crop failures, particularly in the wheat-growing regions of the country.

Poor farming practices also contributed to the crop failures. The Soviet Union used a system of collectivized farming, which was inefficient and led to low yields. Government policies also played a role. The Soviet government imposed price controls on food, which discouraged farmers from producing food.

The combination of these factors led to a sharp increase in the price of food in the Soviet Union. The price of wheat quadrupled between 1972 and 1975. These agricultural price shocks had a significant impact on the Soviet economy. They led to inflation, food shortages, and social unrest. The Soviet government was eventually forced to import food to meet the needs of its population.

Yet another factor that can contribute to inflation is increased government spending over the amount of income from tax collection. This can lead to inflation because the government has to print more money to pay for its spending, which increases the money supply, dilutes its value, and causes prices to rise.

Zimbabwe is a country in Southern Africa that experienced hyperinflation in the late 2000s. The inflation rate peaked at an estimated 79.6 billion percent in November 2008, making it the worst case of hyperinflation in modern history. You read that right: almost 80 billion percent!

The hyperinflation was caused by several factors, including the government's printing of too much money and the collapse of the agricultural sector.

The government's printing of too much money was the most significant factor. In an attempt to pay for its debts, the government printed more and more money, which led to a decrease in the value of the Zimbabwean dollar. The collapse of the agricultural sector also contributed to the hyperinflation. Zimbabwe is a landlocked country that relies heavily on agriculture. The agricultural sector collapsed due to drought, poor farming practices, and government policies.

The hyperinflation had a devastating impact on Zimbabwe's economy. It led to food shortages, poverty, and social unrest. The government eventually abandoned the Zimbabwean dollar and adopted the US dollar as its currency.

Zimbabwe's hyperinflation is a cautionary tale about the dangers of printing too much money. It is also a reminder of the importance of a strong agricultural sector and a stable economy.

Lastly, let's look at how people's expectations can play a role in inflation. People's expectations of potential inflation can contribute to an actual rise in inflation. If people expect inflation to rise, they may start to buy goods and services before prices go up even higher. This can create a self-fulfilling prophecy, where inflation does rise.

Imagine being a young adult in the United States in the mid-1960s. You've never known a time when prices weren't rising. You see the cost of food, gas, and rent going up every year. You and everyone you know are struggling to make ends meet. You start to wonder if it's even possible to save for the future.

This is the reality that many young people faced in the years leading up to the 1980s. Inflation was rampant, and it seemed like it was only getting worse. People began to lose faith in the government's ability to control inflation, and they started to change their behavior accordingly. They bought more things now, rather than saving for the future. They demanded higher wages, which only made inflation worse.

The Federal Reserve (Fed) tried to take steps to reduce inflation, but it was a slow and difficult process. In 1979, the Fed under Paul Volcker made a more decisive effort to reduce inflation. They raised interest rates sharply, which caused a recession. But it worked. Inflation finally began to decline, and people's expectations about future inflation started to change.

It took a long time, but the Fed was eventually able to break the grip of inflationary expectations. This was a major achievement, and it helped to lay the foundation for the economic prosperity of the 1990s and beyond.

This story is a reminder of the importance of inflation expectations. When people expect inflation to rise, they may start to act in ways that cause inflation to rise. This can create a self-fulfilling prophecy, where inflation gets worse and worse.

The Fed can use monetary policy to control inflation, but it's not always easy. They have to be careful not to raise interest rates too high, or they could cause a recession. But if they can break the grip of inflationary expectations, they can achieve long-term price stability.

Inflation can have several negative consequences, including reduced purchasing power, increased interest rates, and uncertainty.

In times of high inflation, reduced purchasing power can have a significant impact on investors. This is because inflation causes the prices of goods and services to rise, which means that your money will not buy as much as it used to. This can make it difficult to save money and invest for the future.

There are several ways reduced purchasing power can impact you as an investor. When inflation is high, the returns on your investments may not keep up with the rising cost of living. This means that your investment may not be able to buy as much in the future as it can today. Inflation can also increase the risk of your investments. This is because inflation can lead to higher interest rates, which can make it more expensive to borrow money and invest. It can also lead to market volatility, which can cause the value of your investments to fluctuate. Inflation can make it more difficult to save money because your money will not buy as much as it used to. This is because the prices of goods and services will be rising, so you will need to spend more money to maintain your standard of living.

To protect yourself from the impact of reduced purchasing power, there are several things a smart investor can do. Invest in assets that are likely to appreciate. This could include stocks, real estate, or commodities. Invest in assets that generate income, including dividend stocks or rental properties. Diversify your investments to help reduce risk when one asset class performs poorly. Rebalance your portfolio regularly to help ensure that investments are still aligned with your risk tolerance and investment goals. Stay informed about economic conditions to make better investment decisions.

It is important to remember that inflation is a complex issue, and there is no one-size-fits-all solution for investors. However, by understanding the impact that reduced purchasing power can have, you can take steps to protect yourself and your investments.

Another negative consequence of inflation is increased interest rates. When inflation rises, central banks may raise interest rates to cool the economy. This can make it more expensive for businesses to borrow money, which can lead to job losses.

When interest rates rise, the returns on your investments may not keep up with the rising cost of living. This is because higher interest rates make it more expensive to borrow money, which can lead to lower profits for businesses and lower dividends for shareholders.

Higher interest rates can also increase the risk of your investments. This is because higher interest rates can make it more difficult for businesses to repay their debts, which can lead to bankruptcy. It can also lead to market volatility, which can cause the value of your investments to fluctuate.

When interest rates rise, it becomes more expensive to borrow money. This can make it difficult for investors to finance their investments, such as buying a home or starting a business. The value of your savings and investments will decrease.

Inflation can create uncertainty in the economy, which can make it difficult for businesses to plan for the future. Inflation can make it difficult to predict future prices, which can make it difficult to set prices for goods and services. It can also make it difficult to plan for future investment and hiring.

This uncertainty can impact investors in many ways. First, it can make it difficult to assess the value of investments. This is because the value of an investment is based on the future cash flows that it is expected to generate. However, if inflation is high, it is difficult to predict what those future cash flows will be worth.

Second, inflation can increase the risk of investments. Inflation can lead to higher interest rates, which can make it more expensive for businesses to borrow money. This can lead to lower profits for businesses and lower dividends for shareholders.

Third, inflation can make it more difficult for investors to diversify their portfolios because inflation can affect different asset classes differently. For example, inflation can lead to higher prices for commodities, but it can also lead to lower stock prices.

As a result of these factors, investors may want to consider investing in assets that are less sensitive to inflation. This could include assets such as real estate, commodities, or TIPS (Treasury Inflation-Protected Securities).

There are many things that policymakers can attempt to do to control inflation, including changes to monetary policy, fiscal policy, and supply-side policies.

Central banks use monetary policy to control inflation by influencing the supply of money and credit in the economy. This can be done through a variety of tools. The central bank can buy or sell government bonds in the open market. When the central bank buys bonds, it injects money into the economy. When it sells bonds, it withdraws money from the economy.

The discount rate is the interest rate that the central bank charges banks for loans. When the central bank raises the discount rate, it makes it more expensive for banks to borrow money. This can lead to a decrease in the supply of money and credit in the economy.

The central bank can set reserve requirements, which are the amount of money that banks must hold in reserve. When the central bank raises reserve requirements, it reduces the amount of money that banks can lend. This can lead to a decrease in the supply of money and credit in the economy.

Finally, quantitative easing is a more unconventional monetary policy tool that involves the central bank buying long-term assets, such as government bonds. This can increase the supply of money and credit in the economy.

The central bank's choice of monetary policy tools will depend on the specific circumstances of the economy. If inflation is high, the central bank may choose to raise interest rates or sell bonds in the open market. If inflation is low, the central bank might lower interest rates or buy bonds in the open market.

Governments can also use fiscal policy to control inflation. Fiscal policy refers to the government's use of taxation and spending to influence the economy. Governments can use fiscal policy to control inflation in several ways. When the government taxes, it takes money out of the economy. This can help to reduce inflation by slowing down the growth of the money supply. When the government spends, it puts money into the economy which can increase inflation by increasing the demand for goods and services.

The budget deficit is the difference between the government's spending and its revenue. When the budget deficit is large, it can put upward pressure on prices. The government needs to borrow money to finance the deficit, and this can lead to an increase in the money supply.

Government transfers are payments that the government makes to individuals or businesses. When the government increases transfers, it puts money into the economy, which can lead to inflation. The government can also influence inflation by changing interest rates. When the government raises interest rates, it makes it more expensive for businesses and individuals to borrow money. This can lead to a decrease in demand for goods and services, which can help to reduce inflation.

The government's choice of fiscal policy tools will depend on the specific circumstances of the economy. If inflation is high, the government may raise taxes or cut spending, while low inflation may lead to lower taxes or increased spending.

Fiscal policy is not always effective in controlling inflation because other factors can affect inflation, such as supply shocks and changes in consumer behavior. However, fiscal policy is an important tool that governments can use to try to keep inflation under control.

Supply-side policies are policies that aim to increase the supply of goods and services in the economy. This can help to reduce inflation by addressing one of the main causes of inflation, which is an increase in demand for goods and services that outpaces the supply.

Several supply-side policies can be used to increase the supply of goods and services. Tax cuts can encourage businesses to invest and expand, which can lead to an increase in the supply of goods and services. Deregulation can reduce the costs of doing business, which can also encourage businesses to invest and expand.

Investment in infrastructure, such as roads and bridges, can make it easier for businesses to produce goods and services, which can also lead to an increase in supply. Education and training can help to improve the skills of the workforce, which can make businesses more productive and efficient.

Trade liberalization can allow businesses to export more goods and services, which can also lead to an increase in supply. The effectiveness of supply-side policies in reducing inflation will depend on different factors, such as the specific policies that are implemented and the state of the economy.

Inflation is a lagging indicator. This means that it typically takes time for inflation to rise or fall in response to changes in the economy. For example, if the economy is growing rapidly, businesses may start to raise prices to keep up with demand. This can lead to inflation, but it may take several months or even years for the inflation rate to rise.

There are a few reasons why inflation is a lagging indicator. First, it takes time for businesses to adjust their prices. Second, it takes time for consumers to adjust their spending habits in response to changes in prices. Third, inflation is often measured using a basket of goods and services, and it can take time for changes in prices of all the goods and services in the basket to be reflected in the inflation rate.

Lagging indicators are useful for understanding the past performance of the economy. However, they are not as useful for predicting the future performance of the economy. By the time a lagging indicator changes, it may already be too late to take action to prevent or mitigate the problem.

Even though inflation is a lagging indicator, a smart investor who is aware that inflation is rising can make adjustments to investments that will help weather the storm. In the previous chapter on the GDP, some examples were listed of types of investments that make sense during periods of increased inflation. We'll look at these more closely now.

Money market funds are a type of mutual fund that invests in short-term debt securities, such as Treasury bills, commercial paper, and certificates of deposit. Money market funds are considered to be a safe investment because they are invested in very liquid securities that are backed by the full faith and credit of the United States government or major corporations.

Money market funds may be a good investment in times of increased inflation because they offer a way to protect your money from losing value. When inflation is high, the prices of goods and services go up, which means that your money buys less. Money market funds can help to protect your money from losing value by providing a safe and relatively high yield.

Some advantages of money market funds include liquidity, the ease with which one can buy or sell shares, safety, higher yields than savings accounts of CDs, and tax efficiency. However, it is important to note that money market funds are not FDIC-insured. This means that if the fund loses money, you may not get all of your money back. Some risks of investing in money market funds include interest rate risk and potential credit risk, the risk that the issuer of the debt securities may default on their payments. It's important to choose a money market fund that has a good track record and is well-managed.

Certificates of deposit (CDs) are a type of savings account that offers a higher interest rate than a regular savings account in exchange for locking your money in for a fixed period, typically 3 months to 5 years. In exchange for locking in your money, you'll earn a higher interest rate than you would with a savings account.

Like money market funds, CDs can be good investments in times of increased inflation because they protect your money from losing value.

CDs are considered safe because they are FDIC-insured. This means that it is protected by the Federal Deposit Insurance Corporation (FDIC). The FDIC is a government agency that insures deposits in banks and other financial institutions up to $250,000 per depositor. This means that if a bank fails, the FDIC will reimburse depositors for their lost money up to the $250,000 limit.

FDIC insurance is important because it protects you from losing their money if a bank fails. This helps to maintain public confidence in the banking system and prevents panic.

CDs typically offer higher yields than regular savings accounts. CDs are relatively liquid, meaning you can cash them out before the maturity date. They come in a variety of term lengths, so you can choose one that fits your needs. The term length is the amount of time you agree to keep your money invested in the CD. The longer the term, the higher the interest rate you will typically earn. However, you will also have less flexibility if you need to access your money before the maturity date.

Some things to be aware of when investing in CDs are interest rate risk and early withdrawal penalties. When interest rates rise, the value of CDs can decline. This is because the interest rate you earn on your CD is fixed, so it will not keep up with rising inflation. The interest rate is the most important factor to consider when choosing a CD. You want to choose a CD with an interest rate that is high enough to protect your money from losing value due to inflation. Most CDs have an early withdrawal penalty if you cash them out before the maturity date. The penalty can be as much as six months of interest.

Treasury Inflation-Protected Securities (TIPS) are a type of government bond that is indexed to inflation. This means that the principal of the bond increases with inflation and the interest payments are also adjusted for inflation, so you are not losing purchasing power.

TIPS are a good investment in times of increased inflation because they protect your investment from losing value. When inflation rises, the principal amount of the TIPS increases, which means that you will not lose money in real terms. The interest payments are also adjusted for inflation, so you will still get a positive return on your investment.

Investing in TIPS protects your investment from inflation by increasing the principal amount and adjusting the interest payments for inflation. TIPS are safe and reliable since they are backed by the full faith and credit of the United States government. They are also tax-deferred, meaning that interest earned on TIPS is tax-deferred until the securities are redeemed. Finally, TIPS are relatively liquid, meaning that you can easily sell them if you need to access your money.

Like any investment, TIPS also have some potential risks. When interest rates rise, the value of TIPS can decline. This is because the interest payments on TIPS are fixed, so they will not keep up with rising interest rates. The value of TIPS can also decline due to market volatility. This is especially true during times of economic downturn. Finally, while the US government is still considered a creditworthy borrower, there is always the risk that the government could default on its debt. This would likely lead to a decline in the value of TIPS.

High-quality bonds are bonds that are issued by companies or governments with a good credit rating. These bonds are considered to be a good investment in times of increased inflation because they offer a fixed income stream. This means that your investment will still provide you with a steady income, even if inflation is rising.

However, it is important to note that high-quality bonds typically offer lower yields than other types of investments, such as stocks. This is because they are considered to be less risky.

High-quality bonds are issued by companies or governments with a high credit rating, so there is a low risk that the issuer will default on their payments. Interest earned on high-quality bonds is typically tax-deductible, which can save you money on your taxes. High-quality bonds are relatively liquid, meaning that you can easily sell them if you need to access your money.

When interest rates rise, the value of high-quality bonds can decline. This is because the interest payments on high-quality bonds are fixed, so they will not keep up with rising interest rates. The value of high-quality bonds can also decline due to market volatility. This is especially true during times of economic downturn. Finally, even high-quality bonds can default on their payments. This is a rare event, but it is always a risk to consider.

Real estate is considered a good investment in times of increased inflation because it tends to appreciate over time. This is because inflation can lead to higher prices for goods and services, which can also lead to higher rents and property values.

Real estate is often seen as an inflation hedge, meaning that it can protect your investment from losing value during periods of high inflation. This is because the value of real estate tends to rise with inflation. Real estate tends to appreciate over time, which means that you can make a profit if you sell it later. Real estate can also provide you with a steady stream of income through rent payments. Finally, there are many tax benefits associated with owning real estate, such as depreciation deductions and tax-free capital gains on the sale of a primary residence.

Real estate can be a good long-term investment, but it is important to do your research and understand the risks involved. Real estate can be illiquid and difficult to sell, and it can be affected by changes in the market. The location of the property is one of the most important factors to consider. You want to choose a property in an area that is likely to appreciate over time. The condition of the property is also important. You want to choose a property that is in good condition and does not need a lot of repairs. The price of the property is another important factor to consider. You want to make sure that you are getting a fair price for the property. Finally, consider your investment horizon. How long do you plan to hold onto the property? If you plan to sell it soon, you will need to make sure that you can get a good return on your investment.

Finally, dividend stocks are stocks that pay out a portion of their profits to shareholders in the form of dividends. Dividend stocks can be a good investment in times of increased inflation because they can provide you with a steady stream of income that can help offset the rising cost of living.

Like real estate, dividend stocks can also act as an inflation hedge. This is because the dividends paid out by dividend stocks tend to increase with inflation. Dividend stocks can provide you with a regular income, which can help to offset the rising cost of living. This is especially important for retirees who rely on their investments for income. Dividend stocks also have the potential to appreciate over time, which can give you an additional return on your investment.

However, it is important to note that dividend stocks are not without their risks. Just like any other investment, dividend stocks can lose value. Additionally, dividend stocks may not always be able to keep up with inflation, so it is important to choose dividend stocks that have a history of increasing their dividends over time.

There are several factors to consider when investing in dividend stocks. The dividend yield is the amount of dividend paid out per share divided by the stock price. A higher dividend yield means that the stock pays out a higher percentage of its earnings in dividends. Look for stocks with a history of increasing their dividends over time. This is a good indication that the company is financially healthy and can afford to pay its shareholders a dividend. Choose companies that are well-established and have a track record of profitability. This will help to reduce the risk of losing money if the company experiences financial difficulties. Finally, consider the outlook for the industry in which the company operates. If the industry is growing, it is more likely that the company will be able to continue to pay dividends and grow its earnings.

CHAPTER 3:
INTEREST RATES

I nterest rates are the prices that borrowers pay to lenders for the use of money. You are probably familiar with interest rates on credit cards, car loans, and your mortgage. Interest rates vary greatly between these different types of credit lines and loans. As an investor, you may be familiar with interest rates on savings accounts, money market accounts, certificates of deposits, and treasury bonds. These interest rates benefit you instead of costing you money, as they are rates of return on investments.

Interest rate values are determined by a variety of factors, including supply and demand, inflation, and monetary policy. First, let's take a look at how supply and demand can impact interest rates. The supply of loanable funds is determined by how much people are willing to save and invest. It represents the behavior of all savers in an economy. The higher the interest rate, the more likely savers are to save money. On the other hand, the demand for loanable funds is determined by how much businesses and consumers want to borrow. It represents the behavior of borrowers in an economy and the quantity of loans demanded. The interest rate is determined by the intersection of the demand and supply curves in the market for loanable funds. When the supply of loanable funds is greater than the demand, interest rates tend to fall. When the demand for loanable funds is greater than the supply, interest rates tend to rise.

Next, let's see how inflation can impact interest rates. As we learned in the last chapter, inflation is the general increase in the prices of goods and services in an economy, which leads to a decrease in the purchasing power of money. When inflation is high, lenders demand higher interest rates to compensate for the loss of purchasing power of their money. When inflation is low, lenders are willing to accept lower interest rates.

Using monetary policy, the central banks influence both the amount and cost of loans that people and companies can get by raising interest rates when inflation is high. The Federal Reserve can raise the federal funds rate to make borrowing more expensive when inflation is too high, decreasing the supply of money to lower inflation. On the other hand, if inflation is too low, the central bank can lower that rate to stimulate the economy and move inflation higher. We'll look at central banks and the Federal Reserve in greater detail in Chapter 11.

Economists analyze interest rates as an economic indicator because they can provide insights into the health of the economy. Low interest rates tell us one thing about the economy, while high interest rates paint a different story.

A low interest rate environment is often seen as a sign of a healthy economy, as it suggests that businesses are confident about the future and are willing to borrow money to invest. A low interest rate environment can benefit the economy in several different ways. When interest rates are low, businesses and individuals can borrow money at a lower cost, which can encourage them to invest in new projects, expand their businesses, or purchase new homes. This can lead to increased economic activity and job creation. Low interest rates can also lead to increased consumer spending, as people have more money to spend due to lower debt payments and cheaper borrowing costs. This can further stimulate economic growth. A low interest rate environment can encourage businesses to invest in new projects, as the cost of borrowing is lower. This can lead to increased productivity and innovation, which can benefit the economy in the long run. Finally, a low interest rate environment can also boost confidence in the economy, as it suggests that businesses are optimistic about the future and are willing to invest in growth. This can lead to a positive feedback loop, as increased confidence can lead to increased investment and economic growth.

A high interest rate environment can be a sign of trouble ahead, as it suggests that businesses are less confident in the future and may be less likely to borrow money. High interest rates can affect the economy in different ways. When interest rates are high, borrowing money becomes more expensive, which can discourage businesses and individuals from taking out loans to invest in new projects or expand their businesses. This can lead to reduced economic activity and job creation. High interest rates can also lead to increased debt payments for businesses and individuals, which can reduce their ability to spend money on other goods and services and slow economic growth. High interest rates can also lead to reduced consumer spending, as people have less money to spend due to higher debt payments and more expensive borrowing costs. Lastly, a high interest rate will likely reduce consumer confidence in the economy, fueling economic contraction.

It's important to understand how low and high interest rates can affect the business cycle of the economy, but economists also examine the relationship between interest rates and other economic indicators such as GDP and inflation. When multiple indicators align and tell a similar story, we're more confident that we're seeing a clear picture.

Interest rates are not a perfect indicator of economic health. Interest rates can be affected by factors that are not directly related to the economy, such as changes in government policy and natural disasters. Additionally, interest rates can be volatile and unpredictable, making it difficult to use as a reliable indicator of economic trends. This is why it is important to consider them alongside other indicators.

When interest rates are rising, the smart investor is going to consider that some investments are more likely to benefit from high rates, and other investments are more risky. When rates are rising, where should you focus your investing efforts?

Short-term and floating-rate bonds can be good investments during rising interest rates, as they reduce portfolio volatility. Short-term bonds are less sensitive to changes in interest rates than long-term bonds. This is because short-term bonds have a shorter duration, which means that they will mature sooner and be repaid to the investor. Floating-rate bonds have interest rates that adjust periodically based on a benchmark interest rate, such as the LIBOR. LIBOR stands for the London Interbank Offered Rate. It is a benchmark interest rate that banks use to borrow funds from other banks on the London interbank market. It's administered by the Intercontinental Exchange (ICE) and is based on quotes from major global banks indicating the rates at which they are willing to lend to each other.

As mentioned previously, inflation-protected securities (TIPS) are Treasury bonds that are indexed to inflation. This means that the principal value of the bond will increase with inflation, and investors will receive higher interest payments. Real assets, such as real estate and commodities, can be a good hedge against inflation since the prices of real assets tend to rise with inflation.

Financial stocks, such as banks and insurance companies, tend to benefit from rising interest rates. They can earn higher profits on their loans and investments. Another type of stock that can hold up during periods of higher inflation is value stocks, which are stocks that are trading at a discount to their intrinsic value. Value stocks tend to outperform growth stocks in high interest rate environments. Finally, dividend-paying stocks can provide investors with a steady stream of income, which can be especially attractive during economic contractions.

Some areas of investment should be avoided during periods of high interest rates. Long-dated bonds can be particularly sensitive to rising interest rates, as their value tends to decrease when interest rates rise. Yield-generating investments, such as Treasury and agency securities, as well as certain real estate investment trusts (REITs), can also be sensitive to rising interest rates. For example, mortgage REITs (mREITs) invest in mortgages and other mortgage-backed securities. When interest rates rise, the value of these investments can decline. Hybrid REITs invest in both real estate and mortgages. They are more sensitive to interest rates than equity REITs, but less sensitive than mREITs.

Additionally, some sectors within the stock market are more sensitive to changes in interest rates compared to others. The consumer discretionary sector includes companies that sell non-essential goods and services, such as cars, clothing, and restaurants. Consumers are more likely to cut back on spending on these items when interest rates are high and their borrowing costs increase. The industrial sector includes companies that produce and sell durable goods, such as machinery, airplanes, and construction materials. These companies are often heavily indebted, and higher interest rates can make it more expensive for them to borrow money and invest in new projects. The materials sector includes companies that produce and sell raw materials, such as metals, chemicals, and paper. These companies are often cyclical, meaning that their profits tend to rise and fall with the overall economy. Higher interest rates can slow down economic growth, which can hurt the profits of materials companies.

As you can see, paying attention to the current economic business cycle, inflationary pressures and interest rates can help guide your investment decisions. As a smart, well-informed investor with an eye on the macroeconomic situation, you can rebalance your portfolio appropriately during different phases of the business cycle to maximize your opportunity for profit and minimize your risk exposure.

CHAPTER 4:
UNEMPLOYMENT

U nemployment is the number of people who are actively looking for work but are unable to find a job. It is measured as a percentage of the labor force, which is the total number of people who are working or actively looking for work.

Economists analyze unemployment as an economic indicator because it can provide insights into the health of the economy. A low unemployment rate is often seen as a sign of a healthy economy, as it suggests that businesses are hiring and people are finding jobs. A high unemployment rate can be a sign of trouble ahead, as it suggests that businesses are laying off workers and people are having difficulty finding jobs.

One way to try and understand the impact that serious unemployment levels can have on individual families and the overall economy is to study the Great Depression. During the Great Depression, which lasted from 1929 to 1939, unemployment rates in the United States reached unprecedented levels, with the peak rate reaching 25% in 1933. The impact of this high unemployment rate on the economy and everyday people was significant. With so many people out of work, consumer spending decreased significantly, which further slowed economic growth.

With fewer people working, tax revenue decreased, which made it more difficult for the government to fund programs and services. In response to the economic crisis, the government implemented several programs to provide relief to those who were unemployed, such as the New Deal. This increased government spending and contributed to the national debt.

Many families struggled to make ends meet during the Great Depression, as unemployment benefits were limited and many people had no savings to fall back on. With so many people out of work, many families lost their homes and were forced to live in shantytowns or on the streets. The stress of financial hardship and uncertainty about the future took a toll on many people's mental health, leading to increased rates of depression and suicide.

Harry Crews' famous memoir, "A Childhood: The Biography of a Place," tells the story of his family's struggles during the Great Depression. Crews' family lived in rural Georgia and faced significant challenges during this time. Crews' family was extremely poor, and they often went without food or other necessities. Crews describes how his mother would sometimes have to beg for food from neighbors to feed her children. Crews' father suffered from a chronic illness, which made it difficult for him to work and provide for his family. This put additional strain on the family's finances. Crews' parents were both illiterate, which made it difficult for them to find work or improve their situation. Crews himself dropped out of school at a young age to help support his family.

Despite these challenges, Crews' family managed to survive through the support of their community and their resilience. Crews describes how his mother was able to make clothes for her children out of old flour sacks, and how his father was able to find odd jobs to help make ends meet. Crews himself worked in the fields from a young age, picking cotton and doing other manual labor to help support his family.

Overall, Crews' story is just one example of the many families who struggled during the Great Depression. The economic hardships of this period had a significant impact on families across the country, and many people were forced to make difficult choices to survive. Despite these challenges, however, many families were able to persevere through the support of their communities and their resilience.

Economists analyze unemployment as an economic indicator in several different ways. One way is by studying the overall unemployment rate for an entire economy as a whole. A low unemployment rate is generally seen as a positive sign for the economy, while a high unemployment rate is seen as a negative sign. Next, economists may look at the unemployment rate for different groups of people, such as by age, race, and gender. This can provide insights into the different challenges that different groups of people are facing in the labor market. They will also analyze the duration of unemployment. A long duration of unemployment can be a sign of difficulty finding a job and can have negative consequences for the individual's financial well-being. Economists also study the relationship between unemployment and other economic indicators. Unemployment is often correlated with other economic indicators, such as GDP and inflation.

Initial jobless claims is a weekly economic indicator that measures the number of people who filed for unemployment benefits for the first time during the week. It is published by the U.S. Department of Labor's Bureau of Labor Statistics (BLS).

Initial jobless claims are closely related to the unemployment rate. A high number of initial jobless claims indicates that the economy is losing jobs, while a low number of initial jobless claims indicates that the economy may be gaining jobs.

Economists use initial jobless claims as an economic indicator because it can provide early warning of changes in the labor market. A sharp increase in initial jobless claims can be a sign that the economy is entering a recession, while a sharp decrease in initial jobless claims can be a sign that the economy is recovering from a recession.

There are several ways that economists use initial jobless claims as an economic indicator. For example, initial jobless claims can serve as a leading indicator of economic activity, meaning that they tend to change before other economic variables, such as GDP. This makes them useful for predicting turning points in the business cycle. Initial jobless claims can also be used to measure the health of the labor market. A high number of initial jobless claims indicates that the labor market is weak, while a low number of initial jobless claims indicates that the labor market is strong. Finally, initial jobless claims can be used to assess the effectiveness of economic policies, such as monetary policy and fiscal policy. For example, if the Federal Reserve raises interest rates in an attempt to slow down the economy, initial jobless claims may increase as businesses start to lay off workers.

Awareness of unemployment rates in the economy can guide you to make smart decisions about how to invest your money. When unemployment rates are high, consumer spending tends to decrease, which can negatively impact certain sectors of the economy, such as retail, hospitality, and real estate. When people are unemployed, they tend to spend less money on non-essential items, such as clothing and electronics. This can lead to decreased sales for retailers and may result in store closures or bankruptcies. High unemployment rates can also impact the hospitality industry, as people may be less likely to travel or eat out at restaurants. This can lead to decreased revenue for hotels, restaurants, and other businesses in the hospitality sector. High unemployment rates can also impact the real estate market, as people may be less likely to purchase homes or invest in property. This can lead to decreased demand for housing and may result in lower home prices. You may want to avoid investing in these sectors during times of high unemployment.

Unemployment rates can also impact interest rates, as the Federal Reserve may adjust rates in response to changes in the labor market. One impact can be on borrowing costs. When unemployment rates are high, borrowing costs tend to decrease, as there is less demand for credit. This can lead to lower interest rates. Another way unemployment can impact interest rates is that it can lead to lower inflation and slower economic growth, as there is less demand for goods and services. This can lead to lower interest rates, as the Federal Reserve may lower rates to stimulate economic growth.

Diversifying investments across multiple sectors and asset classes can help reduce risk and protect against market volatility. By diversifying investments across multiple sectors and asset classes, investors can reduce the risk of losses due to market volatility and protect against the negative effects of unemployment and problems in the labor market. For example, investing in a diverse range of sectors and asset classes can help reduce the risk of losses due to market volatility. Economic diversification can be achieved by investing in a mix of stocks, bonds, real estate, and other assets. Defensive stocks, such as those in the healthcare and consumer staples sectors, may be less impacted by changes in the labor market and can provide a hedge against economic downturns. Bonds can provide a stable source of income during times of market volatility and may be less impacted by changes in the labor market.

In summary, the smart investor needs to know about unemployment rates and the conditions of the labor market because these factors can have a significant impact on the economy and financial markets. Unemployment rates can impact consumer spending, interest rates, and economic growth, which can in turn impact your investment decisions. By staying informed about changes in unemployment rates and the actions of the Federal Reserve, you can make better decisions about how to allocate your investments. Additionally, diversifying investments across multiple sectors and asset classes can help reduce risk and protect against market volatility during periods of unemployment and problems in the labor market. Overall, understanding the labor market and its impact on the economy can help you make smart decisions about how to invest your money.

CHAPTER 5:
CONSUMER
CONFIDENCE

C onsumer confidence is a measure of how optimistic consumers are about the economy and personal finances. It is a leading indicator of economic activity, meaning that it tends to change before other economic variables, such as GDP. Like the initial jobless claims indicator we discussed in the previous chapter, this makes it useful for predicting turning points in the business cycle.

Economists use consumer confidence as an economic indicator because it can provide insights into the spending behavior of consumers. When consumers are confident about the economy, they are more likely to spend money, which can boost economic growth. When consumers are less confident, they are more likely to save money, which can slow down economic growth.

There are different ways to measure consumer confidence. One common way is to survey consumers about their expectations for the economy and their finances. The Conference Board publishes a monthly Consumer Confidence Index (CCI), which is one of the most widely followed measures of consumer confidence.

The Conference Board is a non-profit business membership and research organization that was founded in 1916. It has over 1,000 public and private corporations and other organizations as members, encompassing 60 countries. The organization convenes conferences and peer-learning groups, conducts economic and business management research, and publishes several widely tracked economic indicators. The Conference Board is considered an unbiased source for statistics and trends, second only to perhaps the U.S. Bureau of Labor Statistics. Besides publishing the monthly CCI, the organization also hosts more than 50 public conferences each year across Europe. The Conference Board is a member-driven think tank that delivers trusted insights for what's ahead. Its mission is to help leaders navigate the biggest issues impacting business and better serve society. The Conference Board is independent, non-partisan, and non-profit, and its work is generally well-trusted by economists and analysts.

The Consumer Confidence Index (CCI) is a monthly survey administered by The Conference Board that measures how optimistic or pessimistic consumers are regarding their expected financial situation. The index measures the degree of optimism that consumers feel about the overall state of the economy, and it is based on a monthly survey of 5,000 households. The survey contains about 50 questions that track different aspects of consumer attitudes toward current and future business conditions, current and future employment conditions, and total family income for the next six months. The value of the survey is adjusted monthly based on the results of a household survey of consumers' opinions on current conditions and future economic expectations. The CCI is largely based on consumers' perceptions of current business and employment conditions, as well as their expectations for the next six months of business and employment conditions, income, and the overall economy.

An indicator above 100 signals a boost in the consumers' confidence towards the future economic situation, as a consequence of which they are less prone to save and more inclined to spend money on major purchases in the next 12 months. Values below 100 indicate a pessimistic attitude towards future developments in the economy, possibly resulting in a tendency to save more and consume less.

The results from the Consumer Confidence Survey are released on the last Tuesday of each month at 10 a.m. ET. The CCI is an important economic indicator that is widely followed by investors and policymakers, as it provides insight into U.S. economic conditions and can be used to predict future economic activity.

The CCI is important for investors because it can indicate consumer spending and the effectiveness of monetary policy, such as monetary policy and fiscal policy. For example, if the Federal Reserve lowers interest rates in an attempt to stimulate the economy, consumer confidence may increase as consumers become more confident about their financial future.

By understanding the CCI, you can make informed decisions about how to allocate your investments. One way that the CCI can help guide you in that regard is by highlighting trends. You can use the CCI to identify trends in consumer sentiment and predict future economic activity. For example, if the CCI is high, investors may expect increased consumer spending and may want to invest in sectors that are likely to benefit from this, such as retail and hospitality.

The Consumer Confidence Index is not to be confused with the technical trading indicator with the same acronym. The technical trading indicator CCI is a momentum-based oscillator that measures the difference between a security's price change and its average price change. The technical trading indicator CCI is used by traders to identify overbought and oversold conditions in the market and to generate buy and sell signals.

The Conference Board maintains a website and publishes the monthly CCI and its analysis there. Currently, this can be found here: conference-board.org/topics/consumer-confidence. The report is well-written and extremely informative. Here is an excerpt from the report of August 2023:

US Consumer Confidence Pulled Back in August
Index Erases Early Summer Gains, as Hot Labor Market Cools and High Interest Rates Bite

The Conference Board Consumer Confidence Index declined in August to 106.1 (1985=100), from a downwardly revised 114.0 in July. The Present Situation Index—based on consumers' assessment of current business and labor market conditions—fell to 144.8 (1985=100) from 153.0. The Expectations Index—based on consumers' short-term outlook for income, business, and labor market conditions—declined to 80.2 (1985=100) in August, reversing July's sharp uptick to 88.0. Expectations were a hair above 80—the level that historically signals a recession within the next year. Although consumer fears of an impending recession continued to recede, we still anticipate one is likely before year end.

"Consumer confidence fell in August 2023, erasing back-to-back increases in June and July," said Dana Peterson, Chief Economist at The Conference Board. "August's disappointing headline number reflected dips in both the current conditions and expectations indexes. Write-in responses showed that consumers were once again preoccupied with rising prices in general and for groceries and gasoline in particular. The pullback in consumer confidence was evident across all age groups—and most notable among consumers with household incomes of $100,000 or more, as well as those earning less than $50,000. Confidence held relatively steady for consumers with incomes between $50,000 and $99,999."

We'll end the excerpt there. The report is extensive and continues with many charts, statistics, and analysis of the August survey results. This is an excellent resource for investors and should be part of your monthly research on economic conditions.

CHAPTER 6: THE HOUSING MARKET

Meet Jennifer, a vivacious young professional with a penchant for coffee shops and a distinct aversion to home repair tasks. She had always viewed the housing market from the perspective of a passerby, her knowledge limited to the fact that houses could be either "For Sale" or "Sold."

One sunny afternoon, while sipping her caramel macchiato at her favorite corner cafe, Jennifer overheard a lively conversation at the adjacent table. Two friends were deep in discussion about the housing market's role as a macroeconomic indicator and how it could influence various investment choices. Jennifer couldn't resist eavesdropping.

One friend, Dave, was a staunch advocate for homeownership as a savvy investment choice. He passionately argued that the health of the housing market often mirrored the overall state of the economy. "When housing is on the upswing, it's often a sign of economic growth," he declared, waving his pastry like a flag of prosperity. "This can have a ripple effect on other investments, like equities, as people feel more confident about their financial well-being."

The other friend, Lisa, took a different approach, emphasizing the importance of diversification. She presented a case for renting and diversifying investments across various asset classes. "Sure, housing can be a good indicator," she said, sipping her green tea, "but putting all your eggs in one basket isn't wise. By spreading your investments across equities, commodities, and bonds, you can better weather economic fluctuations."

Jennifer couldn't help but be drawn into their enlightening discussion. She realized that understanding the housing market as a macroeconomic indicator wasn't just about choosing between renting or buying a home. It was about recognizing how this market's movements could impact a broader investment portfolio.

As she contemplated their arguments, a light bulb moment occurred – the housing market was not only a place to call home but also a valuable tool for investors to gauge the economic climate. Understanding this connection was like having an extra set of glasses to view the financial world through.

Jennifer decided to delve deeper into the world of macroeconomics and the housing market. She wanted to become a more informed investor, capable of making decisions that would not only benefit her real estate ventures but also impact her investments in equities, commodities, and bonds. She understood that these various assets were interconnected, and knowledge about one could lead to more intelligent decisions regarding the others.

Her journey into this realm began with questions: How does the housing market affect the broader economy? What are the key indicators to watch for? How can she use this knowledge to adjust her investment strategy and potentially optimize returns across asset classes?

The housing market can have a significant impact on the broader economy. For example, the housing market can affect consumer confidence, which as we learned in the previous chapter is a key driver of economic growth. When home prices are rising, consumers tend to feel more confident about their financial situation and are more likely to spend money. Another term for this is the wealth effect. When people's home values are increasing it can make them feel more secure and wealthy. People feeling this way may be more inclined to take vacations, make home improvements, or invest in other assets when they perceive their homes as appreciating.

Another way the housing market affects the economy is a more direct impact on housing construction and related industries. The housing sector is a substantial driver of economic activity. A robust housing market creates demand for construction workers, materials, and related industries such as real estate agents, mortgage brokers, and home improvement retailers. Housing construction can stimulate economic growth and job creation. Another direct impact is on mortgages and financial markets. When the housing market is strong, interest rates may rise due to increased demand for loans. Conversely, during housing market downturns, central banks may lower interest rates to stimulate economic activity. Movements in interest rates can have a cascading effect on various sectors of the economy, including housing affordability and consumer spending.

For many individuals and institutions, real estate represents a significant portion of their investment portfolios. Changes in the housing market can affect the net worth of investors and institutions, impacting their spending and investment decisions in other asset classes. One reason for this is diversification. Real estate is often considered an important asset class for portfolio diversification. It offers investors an opportunity to spread risk across different types of assets, including stocks, bonds, and commodities. When the housing market is performing well, the real estate portion of a portfolio can increase in value, providing a hedge against downturns in other asset classes.

Another reason people invest in real estate is for the potential long-term gains. Real estate can be a source of wealth accumulation over time. Investors, both individual and institutional, often acquire properties for rental income and potential capital appreciation. A thriving housing market can lead to increased property values, which, in turn, boost the overall net worth of these investors. This wealth can be leveraged for further investment or spent on various expenses.

A further reason some people invest in real estate is for regular income opportunities. Real estate investments can generate regular rental income, which can contribute to an investor's cash flow. In a strong housing market, rental demand tends to be robust, leading to higher rental income for property owners. This additional income can influence an investor's spending choices or be reinvested in other asset classes.

As an investor who is watching the housing market as a macroeconomic indicator to make good investing decisions across a spectrum of investment vehicles, there are several key indicators to watch. First up is home prices. Tracking changes in home prices, typically through indices like the Case-Shiller Index or the Federal Housing Finance Agency (FHFA) House Price Index, can provide insights into the market's overall health. Rapid price appreciation can indicate a robust market. However, if home prices are rising too quickly, it could be a sign of a housing bubble. Declines or stagnation in home prices can imply a risk of future recession and may be cause for concern.

The next indicator to pay attention to is housing starts. Housing starts are the number of new homes that are being built. New construction impacts economic growth as well as materials and labor demand. Rising housing starts can be a sign of a strong economy and a growing population. However, if housing starts are declining, it could be a sign of a weakening economy. When studying housing starts, track both single-family and multi-family starts.

Another housing market indicator to watch is home sales. The number of home sales, both new and existing, is a fundamental indicator of housing market activity. An increase in home sales can indicate strong demand and economic confidence. Rising new home sales point to strong housing demand and future growth in residential investment and construction jobs. More construction spending boosts GDP growth. Growth in existing home sales implies current homeowners feel confident enough in the economy to list their properties. It also indicates consumer eagerness to take on mortgages to purchase homes. When both new and existing home sales decline, it can signal declining consumer confidence, reduced access to mortgages, or concerns about the future economy. This can precipitate a downward spiral. Monitoring housing market turnover provides a readout on consumer confidence, the pace of economic growth, and ripple effects across many parts of the economy.

There are many other indicators in the housing market that people watch. Mortgage interest rates can significantly impact the housing market's affordability. Rising rates can discourage potential homebuyers, while falling rates may stimulate demand. Monitoring the percentage of households that own their homes versus those that rent can offer insights into housing market trends and preferences. High foreclosure rates can indicate distress in the housing market and potentially foreshadow broader economic challenges. Lower foreclosure rates, on the other hand, are generally a positive sign. Rising mortgage delinquency rates may signal financial stress among homeowners, potentially affecting the broader economy and financial markets. These indicators and more can help tell the story of the economy.

As a smart investor, you can use knowledge about the housing market, including key indicators like house prices, home sales, housing starts, mortgage interest rates, and homeownership rates, to adjust your investment strategy and potentially optimize returns across asset classes. Let's look at six different aspects of investment strategy: diversification and asset allocation, risk management, sector-specific investments, geographic considerations, long-term planning, and risk assessment.

First, let's consider diversification and asset allocation as they relate to some specific housing market indicators. Rising house prices may suggest a robust housing market and potentially signal consumer confidence. In response, you might consider increasing your exposure to equities, especially consumer-oriented stocks, to capture potential gains driven by increased consumer spending. Strong home sales can indicate a healthy economy. You may allocate a portion of your portfolio to equities, which tend to perform well during economic expansions. You could also consider increasing exposure to sectors like real estate and construction. Increasing housing starts often coincides with economic growth. You may use this as a signal to allocate more funds to economically sensitive assets, such as stocks, particularly in sectors like construction, home improvement, and financial services. Falling mortgage rates can stimulate home-buying activity. In such conditions, you might favor investments in financial institutions, as they can benefit from increased mortgage origination and refinancing activities. A rising homeownership rate might indicate increased confidence in long-term financial stability. This could prompt investors to allocate more of their portfolio to assets with a longer-term investment horizon, such as bonds or dividend-paying stocks. Finally, for a well-diversified portfolio, consider allocating a portion to real estate investment trusts (REITs) or real estate-focused exchange-traded funds (ETFs). These investments can provide exposure to the housing market without the direct ownership of physical properties.

Next, let's talk about risk management, an important consideration in any investment strategy. How could house prices inform risk management? A rapidly overheating housing market could be a sign of a bubble. In such cases, you may consider rebalancing your portfolio to reduce exposure to real estate or take defensive positions, such as holding more cash or bonds. What about mortgage interest rates? Rising mortgage rates can cool the housing market. You might anticipate potential effects on consumer spending and adjust your portfolio accordingly, favoring assets less sensitive to interest rate changes, such as utility stocks or inflation-protected bonds. Lastly, how might homeownership rates inform investment decisions? A decline in homeownership rates may suggest shifting preferences or financial challenges for potential homebuyers. You might take a cautious stance, considering assets that could benefit from increased rental demand, such as real estate investment trusts (REITs) or rental property investment.

What about sector-specific investments? You can directly invest in companies related to the housing market, such as homebuilders, real estate developers, mortgage lenders, or home improvement retailers. Knowledge of housing market indicators can help identify entry and exit points for these investments.

There are also geographic considerations. Recognize that housing market conditions can vary by location. You might target investments in regions with strong housing market fundamentals, as this can translate into better economic prospects for local businesses and industries.

When thinking more long-term about your housing situation or real estate investing, it's important to consider home prices and mortgage rates. Knowledge of house prices and mortgage rates can inform long-term financial planning decisions, such as whether to refinance existing mortgages, purchase investment properties, or consider real estate as part of a retirement strategy.

Lastly, risk assessment involves close monitoring of housing market risks. Stay vigilant about potential housing market risks, such as speculative bubbles, affordability challenges, or excessive leverage. This awareness can inform risk mitigation strategies and help investors avoid major losses. A discussion about risk assessment and the housing market would not be complete without a quick look back at a recent event in housing that shook the economy.

The Great Housing Bubble Crisis, which reached its peak around 2008, was one of the most significant financial and economic crises in modern history. It was primarily triggered by a dramatic surge in housing prices, followed by a catastrophic collapse, and it had far-reaching consequences that extended beyond the housing market, impacting the global economy.

The housing bubble of the mid-2000s was characterized by a speculative frenzy, as investors, homebuyers, and financial institutions alike believed that housing prices would continue to rise indefinitely. This irrational exuberance led to a surge in home purchases, often fueled by subprime mortgages with adjustable interest rates and low initial payments. As more people rushed into the market, demand for housing skyrocketed, driving prices to unsustainable levels.

However, the bubble eventually burst, primarily due to a combination of factors, including a sharp increase in mortgage delinquencies and defaults, leading to a wave of foreclosures. This flood of foreclosed properties flooded the market with excess supply, causing home prices to plummet. As housing values collapsed, homeowners found themselves with properties worth far less than their mortgage balances, leading to a wave of underwater mortgages and a crisis in the financial sector.

The fallout from the housing bubble's burst had devastating effects on financial institutions, leading to bank failures, government bailouts, and a severe credit crunch. It triggered a broader economic recession, characterized by rising unemployment, declining consumer spending, and a contraction in economic activity. Governments and central banks around the world implemented aggressive measures to stabilize financial markets and stimulate economic growth. The housing market crash of 2008 serves as a stark reminder of the dangers of speculative bubbles and the interconnectedness of the housing market with the broader economy. It prompted significant reforms in financial regulations and risk management practices and left a lasting impact on investment strategies, influencing how investors approach real estate and financial markets to this day.

Before we leave the topic of housing markets, let's wrap it up with another anecdote that ties together some of the concepts you've learned.

Meet Alex, a savvy investor constantly evaluating economic trends. He knows the housing market can provide clues about the overall economy. Alex reads reports that housing prices are rising rapidly, inventory is low, and mortgage rates are dropping.

Initially, Alex thinks about investing directly in real estate. But he recalls reading that the housing market often peaks before an economic downturn. Rapid price increases could indicate a bubble ready to burst.

Looking more broadly, Alex sees connections between real estate and other markets. Strong housing data means greater consumer spending power - potentially boosting equities. But inflation fears may hurt bonds if prices rise too quickly.

Alex decides to adjust his portfolio. He reduces his bond allocation to hedge against rising rates. He tilts toward sectors like consumer discretionary that benefit from housing wealth effects. Real estate investment trusts also look attractive.

Monitoring housing data provides an edge for Alex. He gained insight into both real estate and the macroeconomy. Alex realizes it's not just about making the right property investments. Understanding housing markets helps him tactically position across assets.

CHAPTER 7: THE STOCK MARKET

L uke was an avid birdwatcher and loved hiking in the woods. On a sunny Saturday morning, he decided to embark on an expedition into the dense, mysterious wilderness of the great Redwood Forest. Armed with binoculars, a backpack filled with trail mix, and his trusty field guide to birds, he set off on a journey to observe and understand the forest's intricate ecosystem.

As Luke ventured deeper into the forest, he noticed something peculiar: the behavior of the birds. Normally, the forest was alive with the melodious chirping of various bird species, but today, the forest seemed eerily silent. He couldn't help but wonder why.

Curiosity piqued, Luke decided to consult his field guide. To his surprise, he found a section dedicated to the behavior of birds as indicators of forest health. He learned that birds, being highly sensitive to environmental changes, often acted as early warning signs of shifts in the forest's well-being. Their migration patterns, feeding habits, and vocalizations could reveal vital information about the forest's overall condition.

Luke realized that by paying attention to these feathered messengers, he could gain valuable insights into the health of the entire ecosystem. It was like having a secret window into the forest's hidden world, allowing him to make informed decisions about his expedition.

Much like Luke's experience in the Redwood Forest, the stock market can be viewed as a sensitive and dynamic indicator of the broader economic ecosystem. Just as the birds' behavior hinted at the forest's condition, the stock market's movements provide clues about the state of the economy. Investors who learn to interpret these signals can make smarter financial choices across a diverse range of investments.

So, as an investor, how can the stock market provide insights into the state of the economy? Consider it your economic compass, guiding you through the ever-changing landscape of macroeconomics. The stock market is a reflection of investor sentiment, corporate performance, and economic prospects. When it soars to new heights, it often suggests optimism and growth in the economy. Conversely, when it experiences turbulence, it may signal uncertainty or even impending economic challenges.

Let's explore how to decode the stock market's signals and use them to inform your investment decisions. We'll delve into the factors that influence stock prices, how to assess the overall health of the market, and whether you should invest in stocks or explore other financial instruments based on the market's message.

The stock market is a dynamic reflection of investor sentiment, reacting to the collective emotions and perceptions of market participants. It provides valuable insights into the overall state of the economy, as it tends to rise during periods of economic growth and optimism and fall during times of uncertainty or pessimism. Investor sentiment swings between optimism and pessimism. In a "bull market", when investors are confident and positive about the future, stock prices tend to rise. In a "bear market", characterized by fear and negativity, stock prices tend to decline. One way to remember that a bullish market goes up and a bearish market goes down is to think about how the animals with those namesakes attack. Bulls charge, lower their head, and thrust upward with their powerful neck muscles. Targets of this force tend to fly upwards. Bears on the other hand raise their powerful paws and violently swipe downwards which is exactly the direction prices move in a bearish market.

Emotional factors also play a role in investor sentiment and stock prices. Investor sentiment is influenced by emotions such as fear, greed, and confidence. Positive news can drive up stock prices as investors become more optimistic, while negative news can lead to selloffs. The stock market often behaves irrationally due to cognitive biases and behavioral economics principles. Understanding these biases, like herd behavior and overreaction to news, can help investors anticipate market movements based on investor sentiment.

When analyzing the movements of the stock market it's important to understand how other economic indicators can affect its behavior. Consider economic growth. When the economy is expanding, with rising GDP, low unemployment, and increased consumer spending, investors often feel more confident. This positive sentiment can boost stock prices as companies tend to perform well in such conditions. What about interest rates? Central bank policies, like lowering interest rates, can stimulate investor optimism. Lower rates can make stocks more attractive than bonds or savings accounts, leading to higher stock prices. Finally, let's look at corporate earnings. Positive earnings reports from companies can boost investor sentiment, leading to higher stock prices. On the other hand, disappointing earnings can have the opposite effect. Many traders don't like to hold stocks through earnings reports for the very fact that they are unpredictable and can lead to wild swings in a company's stock price.

As an indicator, stock market behavior aligns with other macroeconomic indicators. Investor sentiment often aligns with consumer confidence. When consumers feel good about their financial prospects, they tend to spend more, which can benefit companies and, in turn, the stock market. A low unemployment rate indicates a healthy job market and increased consumer spending, both of which can bolster investor confidence. The housing market's health can be closely tied to the stock market. A booming real estate market can signal economic strength and encourage investment in stocks. When companies are confident about the economy, they are more likely to invest in expansion, research, and development. This can boost stock prices and reflect positive investor sentiment.

The stock market is intricately linked to corporate performance, as investors evaluate and react to the financial health and growth prospects of companies. It provides valuable insights into the overall state of the economy because a strong and growing economy often translates into better corporate performance and higher stock prices. Stock prices often respond directly to a company's quarterly earnings reports. When a company performs well, beats earnings expectations, or shows strong revenue growth, investors tend to be more optimistic about its future, leading to higher stock prices. Investors closely watch a company's profit margins and profitability ratios. Healthy margins and increasing profits are indicative of good corporate performance and can attract investment.

Corporate performance is closely tied to overall economic growth. When GDP is rising, companies generally experience increased demand for their products and services, which can lead to improved corporate performance and higher stock prices. Robust consumer spending often results from economic strength, benefiting many companies. It can be a sign of good corporate performance and is reflected in stock market gains. Low interest rates can benefit corporate performance by reducing borrowing costs for companies. This can lead to increased profitability and, consequently, higher stock prices.

Low unemployment rates are often associated with strong corporate performance. A robust job market can lead to increased consumer spending, which, in turn, boosts corporate earnings and stock prices. High consumer confidence indicates that consumers are more willing to spend, benefiting companies across various industries. This can be reflective of positive corporate performance and a bullish stock market. A thriving housing market can stimulate economic activity, benefiting many businesses and, in turn, corporate performance.

Investor sentiment can influence stock prices even if there is no immediate change in corporate performance. Positive sentiment can drive stock prices higher, while negative sentiment can lead to declines. Sometimes, stock prices can disconnect from fundamentals, driven by speculative trading. This can create short-term volatility but may not necessarily reflect the true state of corporate performance.

Let's dive deeper into how the stock market reflects economic prospects, the key economic prospects it mirrors, and how recognizing these prospects from stock market behavior can help investors understand the current phase of the business cycle and broader macroeconomic conditions. The stock market is highly sensitive to economic prospects because it serves as a forward-looking indicator. Investors assess the potential future performance of companies, and by extension, the economy as a whole. There are several critical economic prospects that the stock market mirrors.

Economic growth is a fundamental driver of stock market behavior. Investors look at indicators like GDP growth forecasts, industrial production, and retail sales to gauge the economy's potential for expansion. When these prospects are positive, the stock market often responds with rising prices. In addition, the earnings expectations of publicly traded companies are important to watch. Positive earnings forecasts can lead to higher stock prices, reflecting the belief that companies will perform well in the coming quarters. Central bank actions, such as changes in interest rates, have a direct impact on economic prospects. A low-interest-rate environment can stimulate borrowing, spending, and investment, which can be reflected in a bullish stock market.

Recognizing economic prospects from stock market behavior can help investors understand the current phase of the business cycle, which is a key component of macroeconomic conditions. In Chapter 1 we discussed the four phases of the business cycle: expansion, peak, contraction, and trough. During the expansion phase, the economy is growing, corporate profits are rising, and the stock market tends to perform well. Investors may see a bull market as a reflection of the expansionary phase. As the economy approaches its peak, the rate of growth slows down. The stock market can remain strong but may become more volatile as investors assess whether economic prospects justify high stock prices. In the contraction phase, economic prospects turn negative. Corporate earnings may decline, and the stock market often experiences a bear market. Recognizing these signs can help investors prepare for economic downturns. At the trough, the economy reaches its low point, but stock prices may have already bottomed out, as they tend to anticipate economic recovery. Investors with a keen eye for economic prospects may start seeing signs of improvement and see opportunities to "buy the dip" or buy some quality stocks while their prices are low.

Several other economic indicators relate to these concepts and can provide valuable insights. Unemployment rates and job creation figures are key economic prospects. A strong job market is often associated with a growing economy and a bullish stock market. Retail sales data and consumer spending patterns indicate the strength of consumer-driven economic prospects. Strong spending can boost corporate performance and stock prices. Capital expenditures by businesses signal their confidence in economic prospects. Increased investment often precedes economic growth and can impact stock market trends. Finally, the real estate market's health reflects economic prospects, as it involves significant consumer spending and investment. A thriving housing market can positively influence the broader economy and the stock market.

In summary, the stock market's behavior serves as a mirror reflecting economic prospects that encompass growth potential, corporate earnings, interest rates, and consumer sentiment. Recognizing these prospects from stock market behavior can help investors gauge the current phase of the business cycle and provide valuable insights into broader macroeconomic conditions. It's important to consider a comprehensive set of economic indicators to make well-informed investment decisions and navigate the ever-changing landscape of financial markets.

CHAPTER 8: PURCHASING MANAGERS' INDEX (PMI)

I magine that you are a purchasing manager for a manufacturing company. Your job is to buy the materials and components that your company needs to make its products. Every month, you survey your suppliers to see how their businesses are doing. You ask them questions like:

How many new orders have you received?
How much have you produced?
How many employees do you have?
How long does it take you to get deliveries from your suppliers?
How much inventory do you have?

Based on the answers to these questions, you can get a sense of how healthy the manufacturing sector is. If your suppliers are reporting a lot of new orders, high production, and low inventory, then you know that the manufacturing sector is doing well.

The Purchasing Managers' Index (PMI) is a measure of the prevailing direction of economic trends in the manufacturing and service sectors. It is derived from monthly surveys of carefully selected companies representing major and developing economies worldwide. The index shows trends in both the manufacturing and services sectors. The purpose of the PMI is to provide information about current and future business conditions to company decision-makers, analysts, and investors.

The Institute for Supply Management (ISM) is a non-profit organization that provides information and analysis on the manufacturing sector and the services sector. The ISM was founded in 1915 as the National Association of Purchasing Agents (NAPA). The organization was founded by a group of purchasing managers who wanted to share information and best practices.

In 1982, NAPA changed its name to the Institute for Supply Management (ISM). The organization also began publishing the Manufacturing Purchasing Managers' Index (Manufacturing PMI), which is one of the most widely followed economic indicators in the world. In 1988 they began publishing the Services Purchasing Managers' Index (Services PMI). In 2002 the ISM launched the Supply Chain Council, a non-profit organization that promotes the use of supply chain management practices.

Today, ISM has over 50,000 members in over 200 countries. It is a non-profit organization that is governed by a board of directors and is headquartered in Tempe, Arizona. The organization provides a variety of services to its members, including educational programs, research, and networking opportunities.

The Manufacturing Purchasing Managers' Index (PMI) and the Services Purchasing Managers' Index (PMI) are surveys of purchasing managers at manufacturing and service firms. According to the ISM website, about 500 purchasing managers are surveyed for the Manufacturing PMI and about 400 purchasing managers are surveyed for the Services PMI. The survey results are weighted based on the size of the company and the industry. The results are composite indexes based on five measures of economic activity in the manufacturing and services sectors, four of which are the same: new orders, production, employment, and supplier deliveries. The fifth activity varies for the two indexes. For the Manufacturing index, the fifth activity is inventories, while for the Services index, it is prices.

The Manufacturing PMI covers the manufacturing sector, while the Services PMI covers the services sector. The manufacturing sector includes businesses that produce goods, such as factories, mines, and oil rigs. The services sector includes businesses that provide services, such as restaurants, banks, and retailers.

A PMI reading above 50 indicates that the manufacturing or service sector is expanding, while a reading below 50 indicates that it is contracting. The Manufacturing PMI is released on the first business day of each month, while the Services PMI is released on the third business day of each month. You can visit the ISM's website at ismworld.org to view the official reports.

The PMI indexes are widely followed economic indicators in the United States. They are used by businesses, investors, and policymakers to gauge the health of the manufacturing and services sectors and the overall economy.

The Manufacturing PMI is typically seen as a leading indicator of economic activity, meaning that it tends to change before the economy as a whole. The Services PMI is also a leading indicator, but it is not as reliable as the Manufacturing PMI.

The Services PMI is more volatile than the Manufacturing PMI, meaning that it can fluctuate more from month to month. This is because the services sector is more sensitive to changes in consumer spending.

Overall, the Manufacturing PMI and the Services PMI are both important economic indicators that can be used to gauge the health of the economy. However, they each have their strengths and weaknesses, and it is important to use them together to get a complete picture of the economy.

There are a few things to keep in mind when interpreting the Manufacturing PMI and the Services PMI. The two indices are not always perfectly correlated. This means that a strong reading in one index does not necessarily mean that there will be a strong reading in the other index. The two indices can be affected by different factors. For example, the Manufacturing PMI is more likely to be affected by changes in the price of oil, while the Services PMI is more likely to be affected by changes in consumer spending. Finally, it is important to look at the trends in the two indices over time. A sustained decline in the Manufacturing PMI or the Services PMI could be a sign of a slowdown in the economy.

Several factors can affect the PMI: the level of economic activity, the price of commodities, the availability of labor, the level of government spending, and the level of international trade.

The level of economic activity can impact the PMI results in several ways. When the economy is strong, businesses are more likely to be expanding and hire new employees. This will lead to higher PMI readings, as purchasing managers will report more new orders, production, and employment. The opposite is true when the economy is weak. If the economy is slowing down, businesses may start to hold off on making new orders or hiring new employees. This will lead to lower PMI readings. When the economy is accelerating, businesses may increase new orders and hirings, leading to higher PMI readings.

An increase in the price of commodities, such as oil and metals, can lead to higher PMI readings, as businesses need to spend more money on raw materials. This can lead to higher production costs, which can then lead to higher prices for goods and services. This can also lead to lower profit margins for businesses, which can lead to lower levels of investment and hiring. The opposite is true when there is a decrease in the price of commodities.

A shortage of labor can lead to lower PMI readings, as businesses are unable to produce as much output. This is because businesses need workers to produce goods and services, and if there is a shortage of workers, businesses will have to produce less. On the other hand, an abundance of labor can lead to higher PMI readings, as businesses are more likely to hire new employees. This is because businesses need workers to produce goods and services, and if workers are abundant, businesses will be more likely to hire new employees.

Increased government spending can lead to higher PMI readings, as businesses are more likely to receive orders from the government. This can lead to higher levels of production, employment, and new orders.

Increased international trade can lead to higher PMI readings, as businesses are more likely to export their goods and services. This can lead to higher levels of production, employment, and new orders.

The PMI is a valuable tool for businesses, investors, and policymakers to gauge the health of the manufacturing sector and the overall economy.

There are several ways that a smart investor can benefit from keeping an eye on the monthly PMI results. One way is that it can help you assess the overall health of the economy. The PMI is a leading indicator of economic activity, meaning that it tends to change before the economy as a whole. This makes it a valuable tool to assess the overall health of the economy and make decisions about your investments.

Another benefit to investors is that it can help to identify sectors that are performing well. The PMI is broken down by industry, so you can see which sectors are performing well and which sectors are struggling. This information can help you to allocate your investments to the sectors that are most likely to perform well in the future.

The PMI can also help you identify companies that are expanding. The PMI includes a measure of new orders, which is a good indicator of how much businesses are expanding. This information can help you to identify companies that are likely to grow their earnings in the future.

The PMI can also be used to execute good timing of investments. For example, if the PMI is rising, it could be a sign that the economy is expanding and that stocks are likely to rise in value. If the PMI is falling, it could be a sign that the economy is contracting and that stocks are likely to fall in value. By paying attention to the PMI, you can make better investment decisions by identifying the sectors and companies that are most likely to perform well in the future.

Here is an example of how recent PMI results could help guide the smart investor. While this example is based on real PMI results from July 2023, the following interpretation is subjective. It serves as one example of how one might interpret the PMI results.

The latest ISM Manufacturing PMI report showed that the sector shrank again in July, but the rate of contraction slowed slightly. This means that the manufacturing sector is still in a recession, but it may be starting to recover.

There are a few reasons why the manufacturing sector is shrinking. One reason is that the Federal Reserve is raising interest rates to combat inflation. This is making it more expensive for businesses to borrow money, which is leading to slower investment and production.

Another reason for the slowdown in the manufacturing sector is the ongoing war in Ukraine. This war is disrupting supply chains and driving up prices for raw materials, which is making it more difficult for businesses to make a profit.

Despite the challenges facing the manufacturing sector, there are some positive signs. For example, the New Orders Index, which measures the number of new orders received by manufacturers, increased in July. This suggests that demand for manufactured goods is starting to pick up.

Overall, the outlook for the manufacturing sector is uncertain. The sector could continue to shrink, or it could start to recover. The overall health of the economy will play a major role in determining the future of the manufacturing sector.

With a reading like that of the PMI, an investor would be wise to hold off investing in the manufacturing and wait for next month's PMI report.

We explored the significance of the Purchasing Managers' Index (PMI), a valuable tool for investors seeking insights into the current economic sentiment. We delved into the dual nature of PMI, comprising the Manufacturing PMI and the Services PMI, which serve as surveys conducted among purchasing managers at manufacturing and service firms. These surveys provide a snapshot of business conditions and offer a monthly score that can be instrumental for investors. We discussed how several key factors, including the level of economic activity, commodity prices, labor availability, government spending, and international trade, can influence the PMI. By understanding the PMI's implications, you can make more informed decisions about your investment strategies, helping you align your portfolio with the prevailing economic conditions and potential opportunities.

CHAPTER 9: LEADING ECONOMIC INDEX (LEI)

I n a bustling town nestled at the foot of a majestic mountain, lived a business owner named Emma. Her small business had struggled in recent months and she was trying to learn how to improve it. One day, as Emma perused dusty volumes in the town's library, she stumbled upon a whispered tale about an oracle who dwelled high atop the very mountain that loomed over their town. This oracle, it was said, had an uncanny ability to gaze into the future and foretell the economic fortunes of the land. Emma's heart quickened with excitement, and she knew she had to seek this oracle's wisdom.

With determination in her step, Emma embarked on the treacherous journey up the winding path that led to the oracle's abode. The path was steep and perilous, but her thirst for knowledge propelled her onward. After days of tireless climbing, she reached the summit and was granted an audience with the oracle. Emma entered a small and cozy cabin and saw not a mystical shaman, but a kindly old woman tending a flickering flame. She wore not flowing robes, but a simple tunic and shawl.

"Forgive me," Emma said, "but I was told a great oracle lives here, one who can see the future and foretell which way the winds of fortune may blow."

The woman smiled. "My vision is no clearer than yours. However many years of study have given me insight into the forces that drive the economy. Come in and sit. Have a cup of tea and we can discuss these things." She gestured to a desk, its surface stacked high with newspapers and reports on interest rates, unemployment, consumer confidence, manufacturing, and stock prices.

"While I cannot foresee the future, analyzing indicators like these can reveal much about what's to come. They are like signposts, hints of what is around the next bend in the road."

The woman explained how each report acted as a window into economic sectors - manufacturing, employment, and consumer spending. Individually they shed a pinpoint of light, but together they illuminated a broader path.

Emma furrowed her brow. "So you cannot say outright whether hard times or prosperity lay ahead?"

"The future is never certain," the woman said. "But by heeding these signposts, we see the contours of the road we travel. With care and study, foresight can prosper."

Emma stayed for hours, learning from the woman's wisdom. She left with a spark of insight into how to read the winds of the economy. No mystic visions or crystal balls, just a greater understanding of the forces at work around her. Emma descended the mountain no longer seeking a magical oracle, but grateful for real wisdom that would help chart her course.

As investors today, we have it easier than our fictional friend Emma. We don't have to journey for days up a mountain. We don't even need to individually research multiple economic indicators to see which way the economic winds are blowing. We have a convenient monthly report we can freely reference on the internet called the Leading Economic Index (LEI).

The LEI is a composite index of ten economic indicators that are believed to be leading indicators of economic activity. Leading indicators are economic variables that tend to change before other economic variables, such as GDP. The LEI is designed to predict turning points in the business cycle, such as recessions and expansions.

The LEI is calculated by the Conference Board, a non-profit business research organization. The LEI is updated monthly and is available on the Conference Board's website at conference-board.org.

The LEI has been used by economists and policymakers for many years to track the health of the economy and to predict future economic activity. It is a valuable tool for understanding the economy and for making informed economic decisions.

Of the ten economic indicators that make up the LEI, three are financial indicators: the Leading Credit Index, the S&P 500 Index of Stock Prices, and the interest rate spread of 10-year Treasury bonds.

The Leading Credit Index looks at trends in consumer credit and commercial and industrial loans. It is designed to capture changes in credit availability and the willingness of lenders to extend credit to both consumers and businesses. It acts as a signpost for future shifts in monetary policy and the availability of financing that can influence broader economic growth. When credit is more readily available, it suggests businesses and consumers are confident enough to take out loans to invest or spend. This can stimulate economic growth in the months ahead. So a rise in the Leading Credit Index foreshadows potential expansion. On the other hand, if banks tighten lending standards and make credit harder to access, it can restrict economic activity. People borrow and spend less. So a decline in the Leading Credit Index implies potential contraction in the future.

The S&P 500 Index of stock prices is one of the financial components of the LEI that tracks the performance of the overall stock market. The S&P 500 aims to capture trends in the prices of 500 large US company stocks traded on the NYSE and NASDAQ. It includes influential companies across major industries like technology, financial services, healthcare, and consumer goods. When stock prices are generally rising across the S&P 500, it suggests investors have confidence that corporate profits and broader economic growth will continue in the future. So the S&P 500 acts as a leading indicator. Its direction tends to change ahead of shifts in the whole economy. For example, if the S&P 500 starts declining sharply, it can signal investors expect an economic slowdown or contraction ahead. A surging S&P 500 implies investors anticipate stronger economic expansion. By monitoring the S&P 500 component, the LEI aims to incorporate stock market outlooks into its predictions of where the wider economy is headed in the coming months. The stock index provides insight into expected business conditions.

The last of the three financial indicators in the LEI is the interest rate spread between 10-year Treasury bonds and the federal funds rate. Specifically, this interest rate spread looks at the difference between yields on 10-year US Treasury bonds and the federal funds rate set by the Federal Reserve. The 10-year Treasury yield reflects longer-term outlooks for economic growth and inflation. The federal funds rate is directly controlled by the Fed to influence short-term interest rates.

Typically, when the 10-year Treasury yield is much higher than the federal funds rate, it signals investors expect faster economic growth and inflation ahead. This yield spread widens. Conversely, if short-term rates set by the Fed rise faster than long-term yields, it can foreshadow potential economic slowing in the future. This causes the yield spread to narrow. So monitoring changes in this interest rate gap provides insight into expectations for monetary policy and future economic conditions. A widening spread implies expectations of growth, while a narrowing spread can warn of a potential slowdown on the horizon.

The remaining seven indicators that make up the LEI are non-financial indicators. Let's briefly look at each one to round out our understanding of the LEI.

First up is the average consumer expectations for business conditions. This indicator measures how optimistic or pessimistic consumers are about the future health of the economy through surveys and sentiment polls. As we learned in a previous chapter about consumer confidence, when consumers have positive expectations for business conditions, it typically means they feel secure about their jobs and finances. They are more likely to spend freely, boosting economic growth in the months ahead. So rising consumer expectations suggest economic expansion is on the horizon. If consumers grow worried and have bleak outlooks for where the economy is headed, they tend to pull back on spending and investment. This can slow economic activity. Falling consumer expectations implies potential contraction.

The LEI uses this consumer outlook metric to incorporate household views on where the economy may be headed. Alongside measures of actual hard data, consumer surveys provide insight into future behavior. If people feel confident, they will likely continue to drive growth. So this indicator aims to capture the forward-looking attitudes of consumers whose spending makes up over two-thirds of US GDP. The collective wisdom of hundreds of millions of people offers useful signals about the economy's direction.

The second non-financial indicator in the LEI is the ISM new orders index. Remember the Institute for Supply Management (ISM) from the previous chapter about the Purchasing Managers' Index? The new orders index measures the month-to-month change in new orders placed with manufacturing firms based on a survey by the ISM. When manufacturing new orders are accelerating and the index rises, it indicates businesses are positioning to expand production to keep up with growing demand in the months ahead. More new orders imply economic growth on the horizon.

A declining ISM New Orders Index suggests manufacturing firms are receiving fewer orders, likely due to softening demand. Fewer new orders foreshadow a potential economic slowdown. Since trends in new orders tend to foreshadow changes in wider manufacturing output and business investment, the LEI uses this indicator to get an early signal of shifts in industrial production. The ISM combines its survey data on new orders into a single diffusion index. Along with the other LEI components, the ISM New Orders Index helps create a broader picture of where the whole economy is likely headed in the future. So this manufacturing metric gives insight into expected production activity and business investment plans that drive economic expansions and slowdowns.

The third non-financial indicator in the LEI is the building permits for new private housing units. This indicator tracks the number of new residential building permits issued each month by local governments and municipalities. When more permits for single-family homes, condos, and apartments are being approved and issued, it signals increased homebuilder confidence and upcoming construction activity. More permits being issued suggests housing expansion and economic growth ahead. Since housing trends tend to change direction before the broader economy, the LEI uses building permit data to get an early read on shifts in the housing sector. The permit issuance data provides insight into future home building plans. This real estate indicator gives useful signals about expected housing sector growth and overall economic expansion or potential contraction on the horizon.

Next up is the average weekly hours worked by manufacturing workers. This indicator aims to incorporate labor market conditions and manufacturing health into the LEI. It tracks the average number of hours worked each week by employees in the manufacturing sector based on surveys. An increase in hours signals expanding manufacturing activity. Employers need existing workers to put in more time to keep up with growing demand. More hours worked foreshadows economic growth ahead. A decrease in hours implies potential economic contraction. Since manufacturing hour trends tend to change ahead of the broader economy, the LEI uses this metric to get an early read on shifts in factory activity. Manufacturing is a major driver of the economy.

The next two non-financial indicators in the LEI are closely related. They are the manufacturers' new orders for both nondefense capital goods and consumer goods and materials. The nondefense capital goods new orders track the month-to-month change in new orders received by factories for longer-lasting capital goods like machinery, equipment, hardware, and vehicles. It excludes volatile defense and aircraft orders. The consumer goods and materials new orders track orders for consumer goods like appliances, clothing, and electronics, as well as materials used in production like textiles and chemicals. When new orders for capital and consumer goods are increasing, it signals consumer demand is increasing and businesses are ramping up production and investment spending to expand capacity and operations in the months ahead. More orders imply economic growth on the horizon.

Finally, the last of the LEI indicators is the average weekly initial claims for unemployment insurance. This indicator tracks the average number of people applying for unemployment benefits for the first time each week based on state jobless claims data. When initial jobless claims are falling, it signals layoffs are slowing down and the labor market is strengthening. Fewer first-time claims suggest employers are confident in retaining and hiring workers, foreshadowing potential economic growth ahead. If initial claims start rising rapidly, it indicates layoffs and unemployment are increasing as employers cut jobs. More claims may forecast a looming economic contraction. Since jobless claims trends change direction ahead of the overall economy, the LEI uses this metric to get an early read on shifts in the labor market and unemployment.

It's useful and interesting to understand all of these underlying indicators that are using the LEI. It broadens our knowledge of macroeconomics and helps to guide our investment decisions. However, I am thankful that the Consumer Boards aggregates all these indicators into one index and provides convenient monthly reports on their website. Here's an excerpt from their most recent LEI report for the US.

LEI for the U.S. Fell Again in July

(LEI) for the U.S. declined by 0.4 percent in July 2023 to 105.8 (2016=100), following a decline of 0.7 percent in June. The LEI is down 4.0 percent over the six-month period between January and July 2023—a slight deterioration from its 3.7 percent contraction over the previous six months (July 2022 to January 2023).

"The US LEI—which tracks where the economy is heading—fell for the sixteenth consecutive month in July, signaling the outlook remains highly uncertain," said Justyna Zabinska-La Monica, Senior Manager, Business Cycle Indicators, at The Conference Board. "In July, weak new orders, high interest rates, a dip in consumer perceptions of the outlook for business conditions, and decreasing hours worked in manufacturing fueled the leading indicator's 0.4 percent decline. The leading index continues to suggest that economic activity is likely to decelerate and descend into mild contraction in the months ahead. The Conference Board now forecasts a short and shallow recession in the Q4 2023 to Q1 2024 timespan."

I'll end the excerpt there. The report continues with indicator data and charts that expand on the outlook. It's good to know that in addition to the LEI, the Conference Board also produces two other reports, the Coincident Economic Index (CEI) and the Lagging Economic Index (LAG). The CEI provides an indication of the current state of the economy and the LAG as you might guess looks at lagging economic indicators. Together these three reports try to paint a detailed picture of the state of the economy.

Let's consider the excerpt we just read from the July LEI. How might an investor interpret these indicators when considering investment options? What is the overall economic direction? The LEI declined by 0.4 percent in July, following a previous decline of 0.7 percent in June. This suggests a continuation of economic challenges and uncertainty. The fact that the LEI has fallen for sixteen consecutive months indicates a prolonged period of economic weakness.

What are some of the key contributing factors? Understanding the reasons behind the decline is crucial. In this case, weak new orders, high interest rates, decreasing hours worked in manufacturing, and a dip in consumer perceptions of business conditions are cited as factors. Smart investors should pay attention to these specific issues as they can impact various sectors of the economy.

What is the economic outlook? The statement predicts a "short and shallow recession" in the Q4 2023 to Q1 2024 timespan. This is a significant piece of information for investors. If they believe this prediction holds, they may consider adjusting their portfolios accordingly. During recessions, defensive investments like bonds, dividend-paying stocks, and safe-haven assets like gold tend to perform better, while more cyclical sectors may face challenges.

What about risk management? In times of economic uncertainty, diversification becomes even more critical. You might consider spreading your investments across different asset classes and sectors to reduce risk. For example, consider diversifying your portfolios to include a mix of stocks, bonds, and other assets that are less likely to be affected by economic downturns. It may be wise to reduce exposure to more cyclical sectors like discretionary consumer stocks or industrial firms. Defensive sectors like healthcare and consumer staples may be safer bets. High-quality bonds also look more attractive for diversification and income. You might also maintain a portion of your portfolio in cash or cash equivalents to take advantage of potential investment opportunities during market downturns.

One last point to consider from the excerpt is the projected mild and short-term nature of the downturn suggests that completely abandoning equities is unwise. But prudently scaling back risk assets, holding cash to deploy at lower prices, and favoring resilient sectors makes sense given the LEI's warnings.

This is one possible interpretation of the July LEI but it's an informed one. The more you learn about economic indicators the more confident you'll become that you're seeing clearly. This is not an exact science and there is subjectivity involved in analysis. However, when you examine many indicators and they support one another and line up together to tell a consistent story, this can give you more confidence in understanding which way the economic winds are blowing.

CHAPTER 10: CORE DURABLE GOODS

C ore durable goods, often referred to as "core durable goods orders," is a key macroeconomic indicator used to gauge the health of a country's manufacturing sector. Core durable goods orders have been tracked by the U.S. government for many decades. The US Census Bureau is responsible for collecting and reporting this data. Initially, durable goods orders included all orders for products with a lifespan of three years or more, such as cars, machinery, and appliances. The concept of "core" durable goods emerged to provide a more accurate picture of underlying economic trends. The core excludes volatile transportation-related orders, particularly those for aircraft and defense equipment. This exclusion of transportation orders aims to eliminate the impact of large one-off orders (such as the purchase of a fleet of airplanes) that can distort the data and make it less reflective of broader economic conditions.

Core durable goods orders measure the demand for long-lasting manufactured goods in the United States. These goods typically include items like machinery, computers, electronics, and appliances. It provides insights into business investment trends, as companies often place orders for capital goods when they're confident about their prospects. Economists and analysts closely examine this indicator because it can signal changes in business sentiment and investment intentions, which in turn impact economic growth.

Analysis of core durable goods can tell us things about the economy like business investment. A rise in core durable goods orders indicates that businesses are investing in equipment and machinery, which can lead to increased production and job creation. This is seen as a positive sign for economic growth. It can also tell us something about consumer sentiment. When consumers see businesses investing in durable goods, it can boost consumer confidence, as it suggests a positive economic outlook. This, in turn, can drive increased consumer spending. Core durable goods tell us about overall economic health. A consistent increase in core durable goods orders over time can suggest a healthy and growing economy. Conversely, declines or stagnant growth can indicate economic uncertainty or weakness. Changes in core durable goods orders can also help identify economic cycles. During economic downturns, businesses may cut back on capital spending, leading to a drop in orders. During periods of economic expansion, orders tend to rise.

Core durable goods orders provide a snapshot of economic activity related to long-lasting manufactured goods. They are used by analysts, policymakers, and investors to assess the strength of business investment, consumer sentiment, and the overall health of the economy. Understanding the trends in this indicator can help tell a story about where the economy is headed and whether it is in a period of growth, contraction, or stability.

The Federal Reserve closely monitors core durable goods orders as part of its efforts to track the health of the economy. The Fed typically takes a more cautious approach to raising interest rates if core durable goods orders are weak, as it does not want to slow down the economy too much.

There are several benefits of using core durable goods as an economic indicator. Core durable goods are a leading indicator of economic activity, meaning that they tend to change before other economic variables, such as GDP, which makes them a useful tool for predicting turning points in the business cycle. They are less volatile than other economic indicators, such as the stock market. Additionally, they are a broad measure of economic activity, covering a wide range of industries. This makes them a more comprehensive indicator than other economic indicators, such as retail sales.

The US Census Bureau website publishes many different reports and studies, the durable goods report among them. Currently, all the economic indicator reports can be found at census.gov/economic-indicators. Let's take a look at the July Advance Report Durable Goods, in particular the section on New Orders.

New orders for manufactured durable goods in July, down following four consecutive monthly increases, decreased $15.5 billion or 5.2 percent to $285.9 billion, the U.S. Census Bureau announced today. This followed a 4.4 percent June increase. Excluding transportation, new orders increased 0.5 percent. Excluding defense, new orders decreased 5.4 percent. Transportation equipment, also down following four consecutive monthly increases, drove the decrease, $16.4 billion or 14.3 percent to $98.7 billion.

That's a dense paragraph of information. How might it be interpreted if we carefully analyze what it's saying?

This July durable goods report shows new orders fell 5.2% overall, indicating slowing demand and production in the manufacturing sector. However, the 0.5% increase in core durable goods orders, which excludes transportation, provides a silver lining.

The decline was driven by a 14.3% drop in volatile transportation equipment orders, likely representing some payback from strong prior months. Yet underneath that, core capital goods orders still ticked up slightly, suggesting business investment plans remain resilient for now.

This implies manufacturing is decelerating but not collapsing. The broader economy is cooling with inflation eating into spending power. But positive core orders indicate firms are not anticipating a severe downturn, as they continue investing in equipment.

An investor may interpret this report as a sign of economic slowing, but not an immediate recession warning. The durable goods sector is moderating from an overheated post-pandemic surge. So some pullback is expected.

The path forward warrants caution but not drastic action. A prudent investor might maintain stock holdings in industrial and manufacturing firms but tighten stops in case a steeper drop unfolds. Bonds also start to look attractive to hedge risks. But the steady core orders provide a counterpoint and prevent an overly bearish outlook at the moment. Muddling through the crosscurrents likely continues until clearer trends emerge. This report affirms a watchful but not panicked posture for now.

Like other macroeconomic indicators discussed, the core durable goods report provides valuable clues for understanding the economic outlook. When used in combination with other indicators, the smart investor can begin to see the broader picture of the ever-changing economic landscape.

CHAPTER 11: THE FEDERAL RESERVE

The Federal Reserve System (the Fed) is the central bank of the United States. It was created by Congress in 1913 to provide the nation with a safer, more flexible, and more stable monetary and financial system.

Before the creation of the Fed, the United States had a decentralized banking system. There were many different banks, and they were not subject to much regulation. This system was prone to financial crises, such as the Panic of 1907.

The Panic of 1907 was a financial crisis that occurred in the United States from October to December 1907. It was the first major financial crisis in the United States after the Civil War. The panic was caused by many factors, including a decline in the stock market, a run on banks, and a lack of confidence in the financial system.

The panic began in October 1907, when a group of investors attempted to corner the market on the shares of the United Copper Company. A corner occurs when a group of investors buys up all of the available shares of a particular stock, hoping to drive up the price and then sell the shares for a profit. In this case, the investors were unsuccessful in their attempt to corner the market, and the stock price of United Copper crashed. This caused a wave of selling in the stock market, and the Dow Jones Industrial Average fell by 25% in just two days.

The decline in the stock market led to a run on banks. People began to withdraw their money from banks in fear that the banks would fail. This caused a liquidity crisis in the banking system, as banks were unable to meet the demands of their depositors.

The panic spread to other parts of the financial system, and many businesses were forced to close. The panic was eventually brought under control by a group of bankers led by J.P. Morgan. Morgan arranged for a loan of $25 million to the New York Stock Exchange, which helped to stabilize the market. He also helped to rescue banks that were on the verge of failure.

The Panic of 1907 led to calls for the creation of a central bank to regulate the financial system. This led to the creation of the Federal Reserve System in 1913 and was a major turning point in U.S. financial history. It showed the need for a central bank to regulate the financial system and prevent future panics. The Federal Reserve System was created in response to the panic, and it has played a vital role in promoting economic stability ever since.

This period had a significant impact on the U.S. economy. It led to a decline in stock prices, a rise in unemployment, and a decrease in economic activity. The panic also led to reforms, including the creation of the Federal Reserve System.

Looking at this period of history is a reminder of the importance of a stable financial system. The Federal Reserve System has played an important role in promoting economic stability since its creation.

The Fed has several main responsibilities. They conduct the nation's monetary policy by influencing the money supply, interest rates, and credit conditions in the economy. They supervise and regulate banks and other important financial institutions. They provide certain financial services to depository institutions, the U.S. government, and foreign official institutions. Finally, they maintain the stability of the financial system and protect the public interest.

The Fed conducts the nation's monetary policy using a variety of tools. First, there are open market operations. The Fed buys and sells U.S. Treasury securities in the open market. When the Fed buys securities, it increases the money supply. When the Fed sells securities, it decreases the money supply. Next, there is the discount rate. The discount rate is the interest rate that the Fed charges banks for loans. When the Fed lowers the discount rate, it makes it cheaper for banks to borrow money, which can lead to lower interest rates for businesses and consumers. Third, the Fed imposes reserve requirements on banks. Reserve requirements are the amount of money that banks are required to keep on deposit at the Fed. When the Fed lowers reserve requirements, it frees up more money for banks to lend, which can lead to lower interest rates. Finally, the Fed makes use of the Term Auction Facility (TAF). The TAF is a program that allows banks to borrow money from the Fed for a short period. The TAF is used to provide liquidity to the banking system during times of financial stress.

The Fed uses these tools to influence the money supply, interest rates, and credit conditions in the economy to achieve its two main goals: to promote maximum employment and to maintain price stability.

Another important responsibility of the Fed is that it supervises and regulates banks and other important financial institutions to promote the safety and soundness of the financial system. The Fed has a variety of tools to do this, including examinations, enforcement actions, corrective action, and systemic risk oversight.

The Fed conducts regular examinations of banks to assess their financial condition and compliance with regulations. They can take enforcement actions against banks that are not in compliance with regulations. These actions can include fines, cease-and-desist orders, and even the removal of bank executives. The Fed has a system of prompt corrective action that allows it to take early action to address problems at banks. This system can include requiring banks to raise capital, restrict their activities, or even close them down. They also have a responsibility to oversee the financial system as a whole and to identify and address systemic risks. Systemic risks are risks that could have a significant impact on the entire financial system.

The Fed is led by a seven-member Board of Governors, which is appointed by the President and confirmed by the Senate. The Board of Governors is responsible for setting monetary policy and supervising and regulating banks.

The Fed also has 12 regional Federal Reserve Banks, which are located in major cities across the country. The regional banks are responsible for carrying out the Fed's monetary policy decisions, supervising and regulating banks in their districts, and providing financial services to depository institutions and other customers.

The Federal Reserve is an independent agency, which means that it is not subject to the control of the President or Congress. However, the Fed is accountable to the public through the Federal Reserve Act, which requires the Fed to report to Congress on its activities.

The Fed's authority over banks is derived from the Federal Reserve Act, which was passed by Congress in 1913. The Federal Reserve Act gives the Fed the power to supervise and regulate banks, require examinations of the books and records of every bank, prohibit any bank from engaging in any unsafe or unsound practice, and finally take any action necessary to correct unsafe or unsound practices.

The Fed plays a vital role in the U.S. economy by promoting economic growth and stability. It does this by influencing the money supply, interest rates, and credit conditions in the economy. The Fed also supervises and regulates banks and other important financial institutions to help ensure the safety and soundness of the financial system.

The Fed will typically look at a combination of economic indicators when making decisions about monetary policy. The specific indicators that the Fed focuses on will vary depending on the specific economic conditions at the time.

In addition to macroeconomic indicators, the Fed will also consider other factors, such as the political climate, the state of the financial markets, and the global economy, when making decisions about monetary policy.

There are several specific macroeconomic indicators that the Fed commonly watches such as GDP, unemployment, inflation, interest rates, money supply, and the stock market. The Fed monitors these indicators closely and makes adjustments to monetary policy as needed to keep the economy on track.

The smart investor should always be paying close attention to actions taken by the Fed. Take for example a change in interest rates. When the Fed raises interest rates, it makes it more expensive for businesses and consumers to borrow money. This can lead to slower economic growth and lower stock prices. When the Fed lowers interest rates, it makes it cheaper for businesses and consumers to borrow money. This can lead to faster economic growth and higher stock prices.

Another example of Fed activity to watch for is when there are changes in the money supply. When the Fed buys securities, it increases the money supply. This can lead to higher inflation and lower interest rates. When the Fed sells securities, it decreases the money supply. This can lead to lower inflation and higher interest rates.

Changes in the discount rate are another activity to notice. The discount rate is the interest rate that the Fed charges banks for loans. When the Fed lowers the discount rate, it makes it cheaper for banks to borrow money, which can lead to lower interest rates for businesses and consumers.

Another Fed action is changes in reserve requirements. Reserve requirements are the amount of money that banks are required to keep on deposit at the Fed. When the Fed lowers reserve requirements, it frees up more money for banks to lend, which can lead to lower interest rates.

Close attention should be paid to any Fed announcements of monetary policy decisions. The Fed announces its monetary policy decisions eight times a year. These announcements can provide investors with important information about the Fed's plans for the economy and interest rates. Fed announcement videos and meeting minutes, as well as its past and future events, are posted on a calendar on its website. Currently, it is posted here: federalreserve.gov/monetarypolicy/fomccalendars.htm.

The timing of investments and the types of investments can also be affected by Fed activity. For example, if the Fed is expected to raise interest rates, investors may want to consider investing in short-term bonds or money market funds. If the Fed is expected to lower interest rates, investors may want to consider investing in stocks or real estate.

BONUS: MAKING SENSE OF MARKET JARGON

Here is an excerpt from analysts discussing market conditions:

Analyst 1: 10-year yields were hitting 15-year highs just last Tuesday. They've fallen 25 basis points since then. So, rates hit their peak, and is that the green light stocks needed to get back into rally mode?

Let's unpack that statement.

10-year yields refer to the 10-year Treasury yield, which is a benchmark for long-term interest rates.

The 10-year Treasury yield has been rising rapidly in recent weeks, reaching a 15-year high of 4.35% last Tuesday. Since then, the yield has fallen by 25 basis points to 4.1%. This suggests that the market may be starting to believe that interest rates have reached their peak and are now beginning to come down. Stocks tend to do well when interest rates are low, as it makes it cheaper for businesses to borrow money and invest. So, if the market is right about interest rates having peaked, then stocks could be poised for a rebound.

Analyst 1 continues: We start with a major reversal in the rates market, with treasury yields falling to their lowest level in nearly three weeks. The two-year saw its biggest basis point drop since early May. The ten-year now trading with a 4.1 handle, it was just over 4.3% just a week ago. Today's drop follows disappointing consumer sentiment in job vacancy numbers, otherwise known as jolts. Stocks are getting a boost from the yield decline, the Nasdaq rising 2%, the best day of the month. The S&P meanwhile saw its best performance since June 2nd. Have we seen the peak of rates and if so is this the all-clear for a rally in stocks?

Here is what the analyst is saying. The treasury yields have fallen sharply in the morning, reaching their lowest level in nearly three weeks. This is a major reversal from the previous week when yields were rising rapidly. This decline in yield is being driven by two factors: disappointing consumer sentiment data and weak job vacancy numbers. The University of Michigan's consumer sentiment index fell to a 10-year low in August, suggesting that consumers are becoming more pessimistic about the economy. This could lead to lower demand for goods and services, which would in turn slow economic growth. The number of job openings in the US fell by 1.4 million in July, the largest decline since the pandemic began. This suggests that the labor market is starting to cool, which could also lead to lower interest rates.

Stocks are getting a boost from the decline in yields, suggesting that investors are taking the decline in yields as a positive sign for the economy and stocks.

Analyst 2 responds: The dramatic move we saw in rates was something the market wasn't positioned for. We know what higher rates mean for equities, whether you're crunching your discount rate or whether you're looking at the short end, whether it's inflation expectations, you have to ask why did rates go up so dramatically like they did? Is it because inflation is going higher soon, is it a Fitch downgrade, or is it supply-demand dynamics, the refunding schedule, and rates around the world? None of these things are going to get better soon so I'm guessing rates are going to hold at this level for a while.

There is plenty of jargon packed in that dense statement. Let's analyze it.

The recent sharp rise in treasury yields was a surprise to the market, and investors are still trying to figure out what caused it.

The impact of higher interest rates on equities is well-known. Whether you are calculating the discount rate or looking at the short end of the yield curve, the impact is the same. The discount rate is the rate used to calculate the present value of future cash flows. When interest rates rise, the discount rate also rises, which means that the present value of future cash flows falls. This makes stocks less attractive to investors, as they are worth less when discounted at a higher rate.

The short end of the yield curve is the part of the yield curve that includes short-term Treasury securities, such as Treasury bills. When interest rates rise, the short end of the yield curve also rises. This makes it more expensive for businesses to borrow money in the short term, which can hurt their profits and stock prices.

In other words, higher interest rates make it more expensive for businesses to borrow money and invest, which can hurt their profits and stock prices. This is why higher interest rates are generally seen as bad for equities.

There are several possibilities or combinations of reasons. First, we have inflation expectations. Inflation has been running hot in recent months, and some investors are worried that it could get out of control. This could lead to higher interest rates, as the Federal Reserve tries to cool the economy. Next, there is the Fitch downgrade. The rating agency Fitch recently downgraded the US government's credit rating, which could also lead to higher interest rates. The mention of supply-demand dynamics refers to the expectation that the US government will issue a lot of debt in the coming months, which could put upward pressure on yields. The Treasury Department's quarterly refunding schedule outlines the dates on which the Treasury will issue new debt to replace maturing debt. The refunding schedule is important because it affects the supply and demand for Treasury securities, which can impact interest rates. Finally, interest rates are rising in other countries, which could also lead to higher rates in the US.

The analyst guesses that none of these factors are going to improve soon, so expect rates to stay high for a while. This could be bad news for stocks, as higher interest rates make it more expensive for businesses to borrow money and invest.

AFTERWARD

T hank you for joining me on this journey to gain a deeper understanding of how macroeconomics can empower smarter investing. It has been my sincere pleasure to distill these complex concepts into clear, actionable lessons that everyday investors like you and me can apply in the real world.

If you found this book helpful, I would be incredibly grateful if you could take a moment to leave a review. As an independent author, reader feedback helps new audiences discover the book and provides motivation to keep writing on these topics. Please consider sharing your honest thoughts.

The world of investing and economics is rich, complex, and ever-evolving. My goal is to equip you with timeless principles and lifelong strategies to build wealth. But true understanding requires an ongoing commitment to learning. Let this book be one step in what will hopefully be a lifelong pursuit of knowledge.

Thank you again for reading. Here's wishing you prosperity and success on your investment journey. Never stop striving, learning, and growing. The brightest futures belong to those who engage fully in the fascinating world around them.

All the best,
Dan Hartshorn

Printed in Great Britain
by Amazon

36867194R00056